Glorious
BACK NINE

How to Find Your Dream Golf Home

BY LARRY GAVRICH

Round Pencil Publishing
Vernon, Connecticut

Cover: Front: Retired attorney Richard Liberth blasts out of a bunker at his home course at The Landings in Savannah.
Back: Lisa Liberth makes an approach shot at the same course.

Glorious Back Nine
How to Find Your Dream Golf Home

Copyright © 2020 by Larry Gavrich. All rights reserved.

For information contact :
Larry Gavrich
5 Millstone Drive
Avon, CT 06001
http://www.golfcommunityreviews.com

Cover design by David Linde, Emerge Design Group
ISBN: 978-1-7357657-0-9

No part of this publication may be reproduced, stored in a retrieval system, or transmitted in any form or by any means, electronic, mechanical, photocopying, recording, scanning, or otherwise, without the prior written permission of the author.

Limit of Liability/Disclaimer of Warranty: This publication is designed to provide a presentation of the author's opinions regarding the subject matter covered. It is sold with the understanding that neither the author nor the publisher is engaged through this publication in rendering real estate, legal, investment, accounting, financial planning, retirement planning or other professional services. While the publisher and author have used their best efforts in preparing this book, they make no representations or warranties with respect to the accuracy or completeness of the contents of this book and specifically disclaim any implied warranties of merchantability or fitness for a particular purpose. The advice and strategies contained herein may not be suitable for your situation. You should consult with a professional when appropriate. Neither the publisher nor the author shall be liable for any loss of profit or any other commercial damages, including but not limited to special, incidental, consequential, personal, or other damages. Although the author and publisher have made every reasonable effort to ensure that the information in this book was correct at publication, the author and publisher do not assume and hereby disclaim any liability to any party for any loss, damage, or unanticipated results caused by errors or omissions, whether such errors or omissions result from negligence, accident, or any other cause.

First Edition: October 2020

10 9 8 7 6 5 4 3 2 1

About the Author

After a 35-year career in corporate communication, Larry Gavrich retired before his 60th birthday and combined two of his loves—golf and the written word—with a late-in-life passion, real estate. That mix of interests led to the creation of *Home On The Course*, an advisory service designed to assist his fellow Baby Boomers and anyone else looking to relocate from cold winter weather to a golf-oriented home in the Southeast. Over the last 15 years, Larry has successfully matched hundreds of couples and singles with their dream homes in the region.

To build his expertise, Larry has visited nearly 200 golf communities from Delaware south to Florida, plus a few in Alabama, Tennessee and Texas. He has interviewed numerous developers, real estate professionals, golf pros and general managers and written more than 1,000 articles and objective reviews about golf communities, many of them at his website, GolfCommunityReviews.com, and in his free monthly newsletter, *Home On The Course*. For publications like *Carolina Living* and *New England Golf* magazine, Larry has also shared observations about retirement golf lifestyles, emerging trends in golf real estate, insights into club membership and a wide range of other considerations for those for whom golf will be an important leisure activity.

Mindful that, on average, more than half those who live in a golf community do not play golf, Larry has also assisted clients for whom the beautiful landscaping, open green spaces and general financial stability of well-run golf communities are strong preferences.

A 1971 graduate of Rutgers University with a BA in English, and a former Vice President of Communication for a Fortune 50 global corporation, Larry resides in Connecticut with his wife, Connie, and their energetic dog, Coco. Their three married children are Michael, an accountant; Tim, a senior writer for *Golf Advisor*, a golf travel publication owned by The Golf Channel; and Jennie, a social worker.

Larry and Connie also own a vacation condo in Pawleys Island, SC, on a Jack Nicklaus golf course. From there, Larry is in a good position to reach many of the best golf communities in the east and continue to update his knowledge about the market.

Larry can be contacted at editor@homeonthecourse.com

CONTENTS

Preface
Time To Get A Move On 1

Introduction
The Case For Buying A Golf Home Now 5
    Living the Dream 6
    A Few Words About Arizona 7
    Coast to Mountains, and Much in Between 8
    A Few Resources to Help Get You Going 9

Chapter One
Let The Search Begin 11
    Four Seasons, Two Seasons or One 12
    Natural Disasters, Unnatural Fears 13
    Lifestyle Question: Urban, Suburban or Rural? 16
    Getting to the Grandkids, and Getting Them to You 18
    Island Living: Pass the Remote 19
    Don't Overtax Yourself About Taxes 20
    Create a Checklist 22
    Combine Club Membership and House Budgets 23
    Discuss, But Don't Decide to Build Just Yet 23
    Consider the Long Haul 24

Chapter Two
The Internet Search 25
    Mapping Out the Approach 26
    Internet: Blessing and Curse 26
    Just the Facts Please 27
    Don't Fall In Love with Rankings 28
    Sources for State-by-State Comparisons 29

Chapter Three
Choosing A Real Estate Pro 31
- How to Identify Your Real Estate Agent 31
- Valuable Information at No Cost 33

Chapter Four
Location = Lifestyle 35
- Commitment is Better than Involvement 35
- Vested Interests 36
- How Safe Is Your Investment? 37
- Total Up All the Costs 39
- Making the Numbers Work for You 40
- Living Close to the Action 41
- Purchase, with an Option to Rent Out 42
- Acting Your Age...Or Not 44

Chapter Five
Choosing the Golf Course(s) 47
- Extra Golf Courses Add Variety...and Cost 47
- Access to Hundreds of Other Courses 48
- Carting Yourself Around 49
- On Course for Growing Old 50

Chapter Six
The Essence Of A Community 51
- The Likability Factor 52
- A Few Key Questions to Ask During Your Visit 53
- Getting Bugged 56

Chapter Seven
To Belong Or Not Belong 57
- Intangible Reason to Join the Club 58
- Equity vs Non-Equity Memberships 59
- Which Clubs are Safest 61
- Deep-Pocketed Developers Imply Security 62
- Mandatory Memberships Make Scary Sense 62
- Cliffs Dwellers' Revised Plan 64
- Getting to Know the Club Before You Join 66
- The Public Option 67

Chapter Eight
Perhaps Start With A Vacation Home 69

- Resort Areas Good for Rentals 69
- To Rent Out or Not.. 70
- Dual-Season Resort Areas are Best for Rentals 71
- Two-Home Solution..72
- The Option of Condo Ownership..73
- Exchange Your Home, See the World 73

Chapter Nine
A View To A Thrill..75

- What You See is What You Pay For 76
- Float Your Boat...or Canoe 76
- Marsh Ado About Nothing 79

Chapter Ten
To Build Or Not To Build..81

- Costs to Build Have Skyrocketed 81
- What You Should Expect to Pay for New............................... 83
- Yet Land is Still Relatively Cheap... 83
- A Real Life Story of a Couple that Built 84

Chapter Eleven
The Home Stretch..87

- You Know What You Want. Grab It. 88
- An Organized Approach, a Quick Decision 88

Afterword
You Did It...91

Appendix A
Top Communties in the Southeast 95

- Virginia... 95
- North Carolina 99
- South Carolina 107
- Georgia 120
- Florida 124

Appendix B
Supportive Information 131

    Comparisons State to State 131
    Pre-Retirement and Retiree Financial Issues 132
    Mapping Out an Itinerary 132

Appendix C
Helpful Reminders 133

    Buyer Agents' Responsibilities 133
    Key Golf Community Documents to Review 134

Appendix D
Your Home Search Checklist 135

    Choose One Geographic Location 135
    Choose One General Location 135
    What Kind of View Would You Like from Your House? 136
    Preferred # of Golf Courses on Site 136
    Real Estate Budget 136
    Carrying Costs Budget 136
    Narrow Location by State 137
    Desired In-Community Services 138
    Desired Nearby Services 139

Acknowledgements 141

Index 143

Preface

> VLADIMIR: It's the start that's difficult.
> ESTRAGON: You can start from anything.
> VLADIMIR: Yes, but you have to decide.
> Waiting for Godot—Beckett

Time To Get A Move On

I write this at the height of the Coronavirus epidemic of 2020. Like every other American and global citizen, I am hoping for a speedy end to the crisis but am well aware that the after-effects to the economy and our social behaviors may change substantially. In the first six months of the pandemic, we saw an explosion in the popularity of golf as recreation-starved people of all ages sought safe outlets for their needs for fresh air, exercise and social integration. Folks, especially those most vulnerable to Covid, have fled the cities for the more friendly confines of the suburbs and beyond. Employees sent home by their companies to work remotely may stay there for good as their employers realize they are even more productive outside the distractions of the office and less expensive to support with leases and utility costs. How long will it be before those employees realize they and their families can live in year-round warm climates at half the cost of living of the colder North?

That may seem like speculation at this point, but one thing I am sure of, as a Baby Boomer and a golfer: Those of us who are 60-plus are going to move ahead with our retirement plans at the soonest possible time. And that means the migration to warmer weather and an active lifestyle will accelerate after the all-clear sign, if not sooner.

We are not getting any younger, and properties in the top golf communities in the Southeast and the rest of the Sunbelt are not getting any cheaper. Prices in most of the hundreds of golf communities I have followed since 2005 have increased a total of 50% on average over that time and as much as 8% annually in recent years (before the pandemic of 2020). Developers, some still bruised from the 2008 recession, have not fully met the housing needs of the tidal wave of Baby Boomers moving to warmer climates.

An inventory shortage in many of the most popular locations has put pressure on pricing and will continue to do so, barring further economic upheaval beyond COVID-19, until the last of the Baby Boomer generation heads south in 2035. Healthier older citizens are staying active and remaining in their golf community homes longer than did their cohorts years earlier, further exacerbating the inventory shortages. And many millennials who play golf will move South since they will be working from home, and a lower cost of living and warmer climate will provide opportunities to play the game they love year-round.

With savings accounts and other conservative personal investments still yielding less than 2% annually, as of this writing, the purchase of a home in the Southeast U.S., arguably the most popular region in the country for golf, is a matter of timing—and the best timing seems to be now. As I write this in the summer of 2020, the world's economy has pretty much come to a full stop because of coronavirus but, by 2021, Baby Boomers will begin again their marches toward warmer climes. They might very well be joined by "refugees" from cities who have been spooked by Covid-19 and fear the effects of future pandemics. Many of these refugees will be newly working at home, encouraged by their firms to work remotely, not only for their personal safety but also for the huge amounts businesses will save on rent and utilities costs. It could get crowded on the migration highways from urban areas to less densely populated areas, and from the North to the South. Those who prepare and start searching soon will find the most choices and the best prices. Those who delay will likely lose buying power.

If you have been considering a move to a warm-weather area featuring plenty of golf to go with the extra days of sunshine, then what are you waiting for? It can't be cost of living, because you will be able to "finance" your move with lower annual expenses—in some cases, much lower. For example, couples accustomed to spending, say, $100,000 annually on all their expenses—real estate, food, transportation, entertainment, medical and more—could save as much as $40,000 just by moving to some lower-cost areas in the South. Apply that 40% savings to whatever your annual budget is and you have an idea of what kind of lifestyle you can enjoy.

The chart below compares cost of living in three popular golf retirement towns in the Southeast with that of the suburban town of Morristown, NJ, population 20,000. The cost of living calculations do not include property taxes which are displayed separately and based on a home valued at $300,000. The property tax on a $300,000 Morristown home is $6,465. (Note: To calculate the tax rate in any of these three towns, divide the property tax amount by $300,000. You can then apply the resulting figure to any house value in those towns.)

Cost of Living Comparison

Moving From Morristown, NJ to...	Savannah	Mt. Pleasant (Charleston)	Greenville, SC
Cost of Living	-27%	-20%	-23%
Annual Prop. Tax	$2,340	$1,254	$1,980

Source: Nerdwallet.com

Those who relocate to the Southeast will find dramatically lower property taxes in most areas compared with the major urban and suburban areas of the North. One additional example will reinforce the point: The median 2,500 square foot house in Stamford, CT, is worth $650,000 (based on average values per square foot). A 2,500 square foot house in Aiken, SC, is priced at $270,000. Annual property taxes on these dwellings: Stamford, $6,987.50; Aiken $644.00. You may have been willing to pay those New England property taxes, which typically support public education, when your children were attending school. But despite the notion that well supported school systems prop up real estate values, only the most altruistic among us will feel the same about such a "donation" once our children are grown and moved away.

If your personal situation and the current market conditions convince you that the time is coming soon to make the move you have been planning casually for years, read on.

Introduction

> *And suddenly you know: It's time to start something new and trust the magic of beginnings.*
> —Meister Eckhart

The Case For Buying A Golf Home Now

Over the last decade and a half, I have worked with hundreds of couples and individuals searching for their dream homes in golf-centric areas. Most of them opted to buy a home or property inside the gates of a golf community, guaranteeing themselves not only access to a golf course (or two) within walking or golf cart distance from their houses, but also putting them close to a wide range of amenities, such as fitness centers, walking trails and swimming pools. A few chose to live in more traditional neighborhoods, but with a short drive to excellent golf.

No matter where they chose to live, many of them had one thing in common—golf—whether both halves of the couple played the game or one did and the other was content to enjoy the other amenities of a planned development, as well as the social benefits of belonging to a club. In Chapter One, I share some ideas on how a couple should choose a particular golf community when only one of them plays.

Living the Dream

The purchase of a home is probably the largest financial decision you can make, and the thought of moving away from family, friends and all the comforts earned through decades of living in one place is a daunting and complicated proposition, even if the thought of a home in retirement in a warm weather climate was a career-long goal. Children, grandchildren and life in general tend to impose strong magnetic pulls on all of us.

If your dream of a golf-oriented lifestyle is still alive, and continues to be so in a post-COVID-19 environment, then this book is for you. But the ideas in the following pages will also appeal to non-golfers searching for permanent homes where they can stay active and socially engaged, whether on the golf course or not. Retired and non-retired couples considering a location for family vacations will also find ample guidance in these pages. Those already happily ensconced in a golf community will likely find validating information here as well; and those few who regret their choice of a golf community could very well find a way to put things right and move on.

The specific geographic focus of this book is the Southeast Region, an area that is home to many hundreds of golf communities—thousands when Florida is included—and nearly 200 that the author has visited and evaluated at GolfCommunityReviews.com and in other publications. Those communities span an area from Virginia through the mountains of The Carolinas and Georgia, to the Low Country of the Carolinas, the Georgia coast, Alabama and Tennessee, as well as much of the 1,350 miles of Florida's coastline. Moving-company surveys, the most reliable annual gauge of relocations, show most migration in America in 2019 was from the North and

Midwest to the Southeast and Southwest—in other words from cold winters to warmer ones.

In between coasts and mountains lie many golf communities located on lakes and in some of the most interesting flatland areas of the country, for example the Sandhills of North Carolina, home to Pinehurst and its more than a dozen superb golf courses. Although we focus on the Southeast, the experiences and lessons of this book will apply to a search for a golf-oriented home anywhere in the Southern U.S., whether golf is a primary or secondary goal.

A Few Words About Arizona

Arizona residents are fond of saying, "Yes, it's hot here, but it is dry heat." Still, relentless 100-degree days in July and August add up to discomfort, very early morning tee times and 1/6th of the year spent largely indoors. The point here is not to compare Arizona's climate unfavorably to, say, Florida's—it isn't unfavorable—but to indicate why the Grand Canyon State is a magnet for many folks from the Midwest and California. It offers mild winters, though not quite as mild as most of Florida, and plenty of outdoor activities, including a choice of 300 golf courses, that are well-suited to retirees looking for an active lifestyle. And when it comes to topography, Arizona has mountains and deserts and much in between. It is, however, missing one thing that many retirees crave—beaches.

Property taxes in Arizona rival the low levels of those in the most reasonably priced areas of the Southeast. Average property tax on a $250,000 home in Maricopa County, for example, where Phoenix and its suburbs are located, is just $1,600, well below the $2,700 average across the U.S. By comparison, average property tax in Greenville County SC, home to the popular city of Greenville, is $1,733 annually, a couple hundred dollars more than the average across the state and just $10 per month more than the Phoenix example.

My focus on the Southeast region in this book is not to play it off against Arizona, but to indicate you will find as much (or more) great golf in the Carolinas, Georgia, Florida and immediately beyond as you will in Arizona, and that cost of living considerations are certainly comparable.

Coast to Mountains, and Much in Between

Hundreds of thousands of dollars may be wrapped into the purchase of a golf home, but the search process is deceptively easy. It starts with a simple consideration that many of us of a certain age studied in grade school and junior high school in the 1950s and '60s—geography, or more specifically, topography, the "arrangement of the natural and artificial physical features of an area." Topography in the Sunbelt drives climate, and climate is the top reason that retired persons in the North seek the comfort of southern winters. (Cost of living and lifestyle round out the top three reasons, and not necessarily in that order.)

Once a couple decides whether the mountains, the coast or a lakeside community inland is their preferred choice for climate and topography, the process of finding a home can move quickly, and without controversy, even if one half of the couple plays golf and the other does not. (More on that issue coming up.)

The next step is to decide what issues in your lifestyle and health profiles, if any, demand access to specific services. If one or both of you suffer from some pre-existing health condition, or if you are perfectly healthy and active and require proximity to many entertainment options, such as a large university for continuing education courses, or a big airport to make travel home and to far-flung locations easier, then a golf community near an urban area will match your preferences. If you are looking for a quieter, more contemplative location, you can find plenty of remotely located communities to satisfy that lifestyle. In general, far-flung communities are also considerably less expensive than their near-urban counterparts in terms of real estate and such carrying costs as taxes, homeowner association dues and other costs of living.

Golf community courses in the Southeast Region range from the coast to mountains and the rivers and lakes in between.

Imagination and flexibility are key ingredients of a successful search for the perfect golf home. Therefore, you won't find much advice in these pages about what not to do. However, I cannot say this strongly enough: Do not start your search by looking for a specific house that suits you. Couples looking for the perfect house on the Internet before they reconcile the issues of geography, lifestyle and health considerations are courting trouble and are doomed to a long and unproductive search. Everything in its proper order, in life and in the search for a golf home.

At the end of this book, we offer a list of communities that fit a wide range of lifestyles…and budgets. Given the thousands of golf communities in the Southeast, I am confident that there are more than a few out there waiting for you.

A Few Resources to Help Get You Going

TopRetirements.com—I visit this site mostly for the discussion among retirees about where to live out their days. The comments range from the articulate to emotional, but they are entertaining and often helpful enough to be worthy of frequent return visits to the site. And the administrators make sure discussions don't veer off into the political or irrelevant.

United Van Lines Survey Results—A truly objective assessment of where people are moving in the U.S. from a company that moves them. www.unitedvanlines.com/newsroom/movers-study-2019

Nerdwallet.com—Follow the money at this comprehensive site with a number of helpful calculators, including the cost of living calculator I cited earlier in this introduction.

GolfCommunityReviews.com/Questionnaire—This is a 10-minute checklist I prepared for my clients who are considering moving to a golf community home. It is a good start with enough questions to get you thinking in the right direction.

Chapter One

> *In all matters, before beginning,*
> *a diligent preparation should be made.*
> —Marcus Tullius Cicero

Let The Search Begin

The Scene: Somewhere in the northern half of the U.S., at a kitchen table, over a cup of coffee—a good place to start the search for a golf home.

HER: "Hon, let's get serious about selling the house and moving to the Carolinas. We've talked about it long enough."

HIM: "You're right. Where do you want to move to?"

HER: "Hmm, good question."

Assuming you are part of a couple, my advice is to not waste any time on a search until you decide together whether your destination will be near the ocean, beside a lake, in the mountains or somewhere else, such as the Sandhills around Pinehurst, NC. If you do not ultimately agree or, worse, agree to search many areas of the Southeast region, forget about finding a home within a year (or, for that matter, ever). I have worked with a few such couples and it was painful—for them as well as me. For all I know, a decade later they are still searching.

The brutal truth is that it will take years to visit all the viable choices on the coast and inland. If one of you wants to live near the beach and one as far away from the beach as possible, you have a problem. The advice here, especially if only one of the two is a golfer, is for the serious golfer to relent on location. There are great golf courses everywhere in the Southeast but only great beaches along the coast (and only nice mountains five hours inland). The golfer will have plenty of choices. Let the non-golfer—or the one who plays less serious golf—make the decision. Happy spouse, happy house.

Four Seasons, Two Seasons or One

Although winters tend to be mild once you get south of the Virginia/North Carolina border, there are significant differences between the climate in, say, Chapel Hill, NC, and virtually anywhere in Florida. For many northerners, January in Naples or any place in Florida is perfect, with golf playable at virtually any time of any day it is not raining. But July and August are an entirely different matter, with relentless temperatures in the 90s and a set-your-watch thunder shower in the afternoon that may cool things off...for about 10 minutes. If you don't plan to have a second home up north for the summer, I suggest you visit Florida for at least a few days in August just to make sure you can stand the heat.

On a similar note, if your plan is to play golf every week of the year, then the Carolina mountains may not be for you. A cumulative foot of snow spread over the winter months is not uncommon, for example, in the mountain communities surrounding Asheville, NC; and although lingering snow cover there is unusual, temperatures typical of a Pennsylvania winter are not uncommon. If you must play golf every week of the year, then Florida should indeed be in the mix, along with temperate locations in the Carolinas and Georgia.

Southeast Average Temperatures Jan/July

City (State)	Jan. Hi/Lo Temps	July Hi/Lo Temps	No Rain Days/Yr
Jacksonville (FL)	65/41	92/73	251
Naples	75/51	93/74	279
Sarasota	72/51	91/73	257
Savannah (GA)	60/39	92/73	257
Sea Island	61/41	90/73	261
Aiken (SC)	55/33	92/72	264
Charleston	60/43	88/76	252
Greenville	52/32	90/69	249
Myrtle Beach	56/37	88/73	257
Asheville (NC)	48/27	84/64	237
Chapel Hill	50/29	89/68	250
Wilmington	57/36	90/73	230
Charlottesville (VA)	45/27	87/67	292
Virginia Beach	48/33	87/72	249
Ocean City (MD)	43/27	84/66	247

Source: Weather-US.com

A few words about humidity. A heat index reading of 104 and above is not unusual on the hottest days of summer in the Carolinas and Georgia. (The heat index represents how hot it really feels when relative humidity is calculated with temperature.)

"I'm not a stranger to humidity," says Brad Chambers, who publishes the ShootingYourAge.com blog and grew up in the South. "Humidity, as much as heat, is a factor from the Carolinas south."

Natural Disasters, Unnatural Fears

You can't escape weather and, with few exceptions, you can't escape the possibility of natural disasters like hurricanes, tornadoes and mudslides caused by torrential rains. Many couples who would like to live near the ocean on the east coast worry about the threat of hurricanes. But in truth, according to the National Hurricane Center, the chances of a major hurricane striking a particular location on the coast are fairly slim. For example, the odds of a major hurricane (winds 111 mph or higher passing within 75 miles) are just 2.2% in Charleston, SC, 2.6% in Myrtle Beach, 2.1% in Wilmington, NC, and just 1.3% in Savannah, GA. Savannah, although on the coast, is located well to the west of the Florida and Carolinas coastlines, and Atlantic hurricanes tend to whistle past the city, well to the east, courtesy of the Gulfstream. Florida's coastline from around Vero Beach south is not so lucky; but still the odds of a Category 4 or higher are between 4 and 10 per 100 years.

Stated another way, Myrtle Beach will suffer 2.1 major hurricanes every 100 years and Savannah just 1.3. Worst case scenario: The Weather Channel will warn you and local officials are well trained to get you to safety.

Hurricane Strikes on SE Coast from 1900 to 2010 (Source: National Hurricane Center)

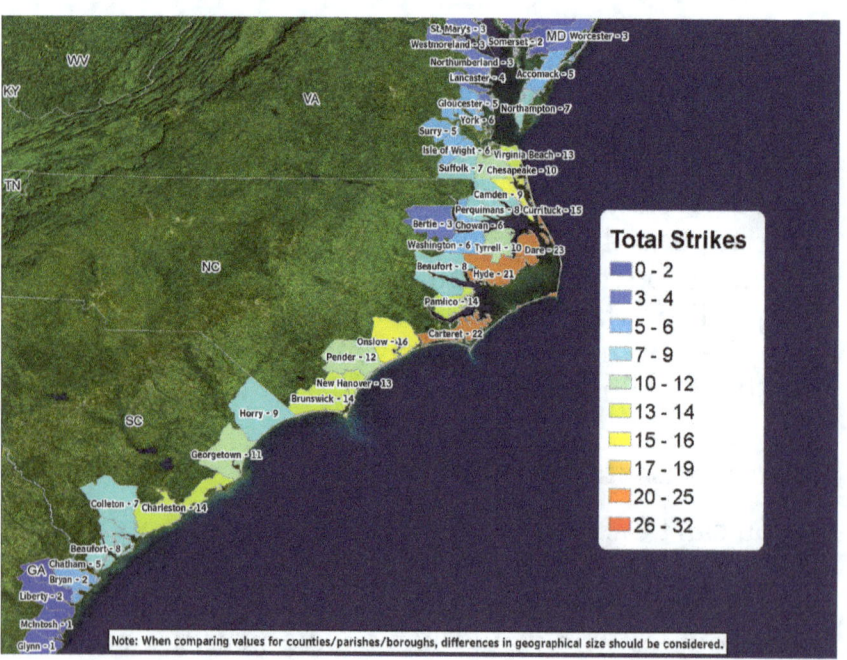

One important related issue, however, is flood insurance, which is required in many coastal locations and a good idea for those who live near, but not in, a flood zone. According to FEMA, "Whether you are in a high risk zone or not, you may need flood insurance because most homeowner insurance does not cover flood damage." If you live in an area with low or moderate flood risk, you are five times more likely to experience flooding than a fire in your home over the next 30 years. For many, a National Flood Insurance Program insurance policy could cost less than $400 per year. FEMA offers a mapping program at its website that will identify the type of flood zone by home address.

Hurricane Strikes on Florida Coasts, 1900 to 2010 (Source: National Hurricane Center)

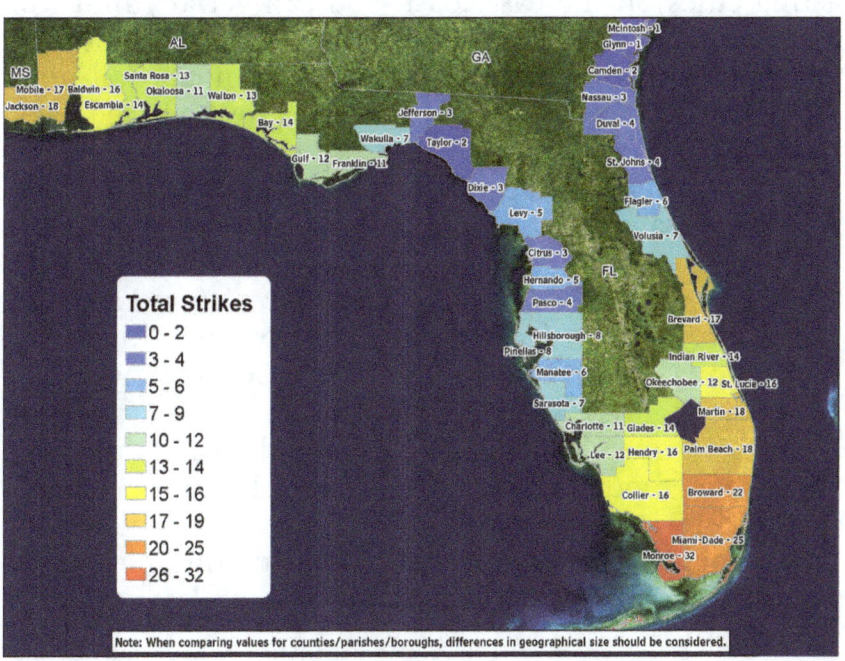

Another excellent source for flood risk is a site called FloodFactor.com. Plug in your address, or the address of a property in which you are interested, and you will almost instantly know the size of the flood risk. Their maps are cool too. As we were going to press, Realtor.com announced that it would begin to publish the FloodFactor.com assessments for many homes for sale listed on the Realtor.com website.

Lifestyle Question: Urban, Suburban or Rural?

In the Southeast Region, you will find excellent golf communities within 15 minutes of cities as well as 90 minutes away, and at all distances in between. Your choice of how far from a city you should live comes down to your preferred lifestyle.

Let's compare two fine communities at both ends of the spectrum in terms of location. The Landings on Skidaway Island in Georgia is a mere 20 minutes from downtown Savannah, one of the most historic and interesting cities on the east coast. You can get anything you want in Savannah, including fine restaurants, multiple supermarkets, museums (the famed Savannah College of Art & Design is a strong presence downtown), a well-rated hospital, a regional airport and a host of other large-city services. Couples accustomed to frequent nights out will find the theaters and dining options more than ample in Savannah.

Savannah Lakes Village is nowhere near Savannah, but it gets its name from the nearby Savannah River. The community, which is home to about 2,000 mostly retired residents, sports two excellent golf courses of different character—one classic and on gently sloped terrain, and the other modern with significant elevation changes. It also offers a full roster of amenities and some of the least expensive real estate of any golf community in the Southeast. Homeowner association fees are less than $120 per month.

Savannah Lakes, McCormick, SC

Located in the town of McCormick, SC, Savannah Lakes is the very definition of "rural," with Greenville a 1 1/2 hour drive and Augusta, GA, an hour. There is only one supermarket option, a Food Lion eight miles from the community. A couple of hospitals are located about a half hour away. Those looking to replicate urban and suburban services they were used to for decades might not adjust well to such a remote location. Yet those looking for a bargain in real estate in a noise- and air-pollution-free environment, beside a clean lake (Lake Thurmond) with plenty to do "inside the gates," will find their niche at Savannah Lakes.

How to tell the difference between near-urban and rural? For starters, a map helps. Check out the proximities of the golf communities you are targeting to cities or towns of size, do a little research on those towns—Wikipedia is a good starting place—and decide if they have what you want and if they are close enough for comfort to a big town, or far enough away for peace and quiet and little traffic.

Getting to the Grandkids, and Getting Them to You

One of the toughest decisions a retired couple makes is moving many miles away from their children and grandkids. I've met some couples who would not think of moving more than a short car drive from their grandchildren; they see babysitting as their major retirement activity.

But the vast majority, who love their kids and grandkids every bit as much, are happy to be in a warm weather climate a good half-day's drive away, which they see as close enough to react to an emergency back home but far enough to remove the temptation to be everpresent.

There is a way to satisfy the desire for a warmer climate and the ability to get most places within a few hours, and that is by moving to a golf community not too far from a good regional airport or major airline hub such as Charlotte (CLT), Raleigh (RDU), Tampa (TPA), and Atlanta (ATL). Even regional airports like Charleston, for example, and Myrtle Beach, offer enough daily flights to major northern cities to put a couple within a half-day return home. (For example, Charleston International Airport provides eight daily non-stop flights to the New York City area and three to Chicago.) That also increases the likelihood the family back home will visit you in the summer.

Total Airport-to-Airport Flight Times from SE cities to Northern Cities (in hours)

	Phil.	NY	Chic	Pitt.	Bos.	Hartford
Myrtle Beach	1.5	2.0	2.5	1.5	2.0	1.75
Charleston	1.75	2.0	2.5	1.5	2.25	3.5
Charlotte	1.5	1.75	2.0	1.5	2.0	2.0
Greenville (SC)	1.75	2.0	2.25	3.5	3.5	3.5
Wilmington (NC)	1.5	1.75	2.5	3.25	2.0	3.25
Savannah	2.0	2.25	2.5	3.5	2.5	3.75
Jacksonville (FL)	2.25	2.25	2.75	3.5	2.5	3.75
West Palm Beach	2.5	2.75	3.25	2.5	3.0	2.75

Flight times from Expedia.com

Island Living: Pass the Remote

You cannot be much more remotely located than on an island with no cars and only ferry service to bring you to and from the rest of civilization. The two best such golf community islands on the east coast are Bald Head Island in North Carolina and Haig Point on Daufuskie Island in South Carolina, just across the Calibogue Sound from the famed Hilton Head Lighthouse.

There are no bridges to these islands from the mainland; residents or vacationers park their cars in a designated lot in Southport, NC (for Bald Head) or on Hilton Head Island (for Haig Point) and catch the community's ferry to each island. As you might expect, a golf community doesn't get much quieter than on an island that comprises retirees for most of the year, except for visiting grandchildren in summers. And as for noise and air pollution, electric golf carts create neither.

Haig Point, Daufuskie Island, SC
Photo Courtesy of Dennis Burnette

Don't Overtax Yourself About Taxes

Three states in the Southeast—Florida, Alabama and Tennessee—do not impose a state income tax on their citizens. In retirement, if you earn hundreds of thousands of dollars, then God bless; Florida or the other two no-income-tax states are viable choices. But for the great majority of the rest of us, the state income tax is relatively meaningless, especially since those states without one have to make up the loss of revenue somehow. (Sales taxes seem to be a popular way.)

The overall cost of living in Florida's cities and towns, for example, rivals that of many cities in the North and is considerably higher than most locations in the Carolinas and Georgia. Insurance rates in the Sunshine State are about the highest in the nation. And former commuters to cities like New York and Boston will relive nightmares sitting in Florida interstate and local traffic, especially during the winter months when the population level of the state explodes. (You can circumvent some of those problems by paying tolls.). Still, if you want to play year-round golf and enjoy the best weather in the U.S. during the winter months, Florida is a great option. But unless you maintain a large income, don't choose Florida for the income tax break alone.

The financial newsletter *Kiplinger* indicates that South Carolina is actually more tax friendly to retirees than is Florida. Like Florida, South Carolina does not tax Social Security income but offers additional breaks to seniors, such as the exclusion from state taxation of up to $25,000 of retirement and other income. The average property tax on a $400,000 home in Florida is $3,920 annually; in South Carolina it is $2,402.

Cost of Living by States North vs. South
Average U.S. Cost of Living Index = 100

State	Rank	COL Index
Mississippi	1	86.1
Tennessee*	6	88.7
Michigan	7	88.9
Georgia	9	89.2
Alabama*	11	89.3
Indiana	12	90.0
Iowa	13	90.1
Ohio	15	90.8
North Carolina	22	94.9
South Carolina	23	95.9
Wisconsin	25	97.3
Florida*	26	97.9
Virginia	30	100.7
Minnesota	31	101.6
Pennsylvania	32	101.7
New Hampshire*	37	109.7
Vermont	39	114.5
Rhode Island	41	119.4
New Jersey	42	125.1
Connecticut	43	127.7
Massachusetts	46	131.6
New York	48	139.1
California	49	152.7

*no-income-tax state
source: WorldPopulationReview.com

Georgia is close behind in terms of tax treatment for seniors. But virtually any state in the Southeast will do, compared with most states in the Northeast and certainly with California (see table above) from an overall tax standpoint; Tennessee, Mississippi, Alabama, Florida, Georgia and South Carolina all rank in the Top 10 for retiree-friendly taxes in the U.S. and are all below the median U.S. level for cost of living.

Create a Checklist

Once you have decided on a general location for your search, you need to have a checklist, for two major reasons: 1) it will make your Internet search for appropriate golf communities more relevant and more focused; and 2) it will keep to a minimum any disagreements about which golf communities you should visit.

Your checklist should include, in rank order, the amenities you want available inside your community, including walking trails, fitness center, pools and others. Make the list as complete as you can because some amenities down the list could tilt you toward one community over another. It is important that you reconcile in advance how far you need to be from such services as a hospital, commercial airport, supermarket, beach or lake, quality restaurants, shopping centers and other services. And decide early on if one golf course in the community you choose will do, or if you want variety in the form of 36 or more holes. (See Chapter Five for more on multi-golf-course communities.)

Of course, that checklist must include a price range for the home (or property) you intend to purchase, and a general idea of its size (number of rooms and square footage). Although I don't recommend it as a make or break feature early in the process, it will be good to agree on the type of view you would like to enjoy from your golf community home. In general, there is a premium of up to 20% in some communities for a golf course view, and 30% or more for a lake or river view; forget about commanding views of the ocean unless you have a couple of million dollars to spend. I explore the view factor in Chapter Nine.

See Appendix D for an extended checklist. Personalize it as you see fit.

LET THE SEARCH BEGIN

Combine Club Membership and House Budgets

If you are not moving to a golf community to simply enjoy the landscaping and greenery, or to watch other people play golf as you sit on your patio, but rather to join in the life of the community, then you need to estimate early-on your budget for club membership. There is a cost to joining a private golf community club, ranging anywhere from zero to tens of thousands of dollars. Your housing budget should include both the cost of the home *and* the cost of initiation fees. For example, let's say your total budget for house and golf is $450,000. That means you could afford a $400,000 house and $50,000 initiation fee, or a $440,000 house and $10,000 initiation fee, both cases relevant in top-quality golf communities.

And do not forget your monthly budget; you will be compelled to pay monthly dues for golf, and monthly dues to your community's homeowner association. (Note: In some communities, you will be part of a neighborhood association, with additional monthly obligations.) If you are not a golfer, virtually every country club offers a social membership at lower cost than the full-golf membership and provides access to the clubhouse, pools and social events.

I offer a Golf Home Questionnaire at my website GolfCommunityReviews.com that is essentially a checklist of the major items you will want to consider. Once you fill it out, we can arrange for a free, no-obligation discussion about which areas and specific communities match your requirements.

Discuss, But Don't Decide to Build Just Yet

If, during your pre-retirement lives, you always purchased a resale home, for retirement you might be inclined to buy a nice homesite and build your dream golf home on it, tired of always having lived in "someone else's house." This early stage of your search is not a bad time to discuss the idea of building the home you want for your retirement, but make no decisions at this point. Rather, wait until you have chosen the community in which you will live and play golf, and then look at homesites and work the numbers. I discuss the new home versus resale conundrum in Chapter Ten.

Consider the Long Haul

It is difficult for any of us to project where we will be in 10 or 15 years, but for those of us in a certain age category, we can pretty much count on mobility and health issues in our 70s and 80s. This is why it is important, at the beginning of the search process, to consider how age-friendly a community could be a decade or two down the road.

Steve Benz, who owns two homes in golf communities, one in Florida and one in Ohio, considered aging in place a factor when he and his wife were looking for a golf community in the South.

"Is the club you are looking at totally golf-centric?" Steve asks. "If so, that could be a problem as one ages. Or does it have other activities that are popular, such as bocce, pickle ball and croquet?"

"In my club in Florida," Steve adds, "I see people with walkers still demonstrating a competitive spirit in the bocce leagues."

An even more important question: Will the hospital just 30 minutes away when you are in your 60s seem too far away in your mid 70s? Will the distance to the nearest supermarket and restaurants start to look farther and farther away as the years go rolling by?

The front end of your search is the proper time to do some "what-if" planning.

"Planning up front," Steve Benz says, "can potentially avoid a double-move and its costs during retirement, as well as the necessity to develop a whole new set of friends."

Chapter Two

> *Google can bring you back 100,000 answers.*
> *A librarian can bring you back the right one.*
> —Neil Gaiman

The Internet Search

In the 1950s, when the migration south for retirement first began in earnest, there was no Internet to guide the way. At best a few slick brochures, and perhaps equally slick salespersons, communicated what each development in Florida offered its residents. It wasn't easy to separate fact from fiction until you paid a visit, and that was not too easy 60 years ago.

Today, of course, with a few keystrokes you can find out just about anything you want to know about an area and a community in which you might spend most of the rest of your life.

Mapping Out the Approach

Since by this time you should have decided on some areas of the Southeast to focus on—mountains, lakes or coastal in one or two specific states—your Internet search terms should reflect those choices. Say, for example, you are looking for a golf community within 15 minutes or so of an ocean beach but also near a city because you want access to a lot of services; in that case, access a map of the coast (e.g. Google Maps) from Virginia Beach south through Florida and another for the Gulf Coast of Florida (assuming a home in Florida is in contention; if not, your search will be more straightforward). Below the Virginia/North Carolina border, there really aren't that many cities on the coast until you get to Florida. The select few are Wilmington, NC; Charleston, SC; Savannah, GA; and Jacksonville, FL, which is just over the Georgia state line.

Internet: Blessing and Curse

I wish I had a dime for every time a golf community website used the phrase "Championship Golf Course." What does that mean anyway, especially when the club championship is about the highest-level event ever played on the course? Ditto the come-ons "World Class Golf," "Welcome to Paradise" and "Natural Beauty." Such vacuous tags front and center on a website are a bad introduction to a community and promise a Shangri-La that only exists in fairy tales.

The hype is the worst part of an Internet search, and my advice is to ignore it all. Skip the "about us" sections at each website—they all read about the same—and go directly to the tabs at the top of most of the home pages that describe the amenities the community offers (often under the heading of "Lifestyle"), such as fitness center, walking trails, the number of golf courses, tennis courts, etc. And try to avoid the "customer testimonials" in which a couple tells you how happy they were with their decision. I don't doubt their sincerity but, again, they all tend to sound the same positive notes one community to the next.

Better to ignore the hype and look for all the must-have items on your checklist. If your requirements match what a particular community has to offer, keep it on the list of potentials for a visit. If it doesn't, delete it and move on. Of course, this begs the question: What is the best way to search for those specific communities that match your parameters?

Just the Facts Please

No rational developer or real estate agency should expect you to plunk down $300,000 or more after seeing a few photos and reading a few descriptions of a golf community. The trick for them is to be enticing enough to provoke the keen interest of couples looking to retire to a warm-weather location, relocate for better job prospects or establish a family vacation spot. The best way to do that is with information, not puffery.

A golf community website should have one goal in mind: Stand out enough to get you to visit. Golf community representatives I have spoken with over the years have indicated that, on average, one out of every five or six couples who visit their communities eventually purchase a property. Those odds are good enough to compel golf communities to spend a large chunk of their marketing budgets on their websites, and to understand that facts, not hyperbole, drive customer interest. I wish more of them understood that.

Scan the homes-for-sale listings on a website only to confirm that homes in the community fit your price range. At this point, it is a waste of effort to look closely at individual homes. They are likely to be sold by the time of your visit and no one home communicates anything about the surrounding community. Fall in love with the community before you fall in love with a house.

You will want an idea of membership costs, but few golf communities disclose the golf initiation fees and monthly golf dues on their websites, nor do they tend to indicate the amount of homeowner association dues. This will be the job of the real estate agents you contact. (More on that in the next chapter.)

If you are a golfer, try to fast forward a decade or two and consider the golf communities you are looking at in terms of activities beyond golf. There may come a time when you age beyond golf; if so, activities like bocce, pickle ball or croquet might feed your competitiveness. Most golf communities will list on their web sites the activities that are senior friendly; if they don't, ask with an email or phone call to their sales office.

There are many extremely helpful websites to assist you in your search. (I list a few below and in Appendix B.) Some will compare cities by cost of living and property tax rates; others will provide demographic and census data on specific cities; golf course review sites can provide some idea of course conditions and playability; and some sites will rank nearby hospitals by their quality of care, useful for those of us with ongoing medical needs.

Don't Fall In Love with Rankings

Beware, though, of magazines and online websites that disguise themselves as objective but are really designed to tout communities that pay them a marketing fee and/or advertise in their pages. A popular magazine like *Where to Retire* can provide some helpful data, such as its cost of living chart that compares cities north and south. However, avoid articles such as their "Top 50 Communities," a list that tracks way too closely with their top advertisers to offer a fully objective ranking. (Some of the communities left off their list are inarguably worthy of Top 50 status.) Other magazines sponsor trade shows and also tend to tilt toward those developments that rent booths at their shows and advertise in their magazines.

THE INTERNET SEARCH

You can spread your Internet research on golf communities over a few days but, in the aggregate, and if you have targeted just a handful of geographic locations, count on five hours or so.

Sources for State-by-State Comparisons

Kiplinger.com—Excellent, easy to follow advice and comparisons of states by their overall taxation rates, not just income tax.

BestPlaces.net—Using census and other data, compares cities by their cost of living rates and other factors. However, the richest benefit from the data now requires a paid subscription.

https://www.best-place-to-retire.com/places-to-retire-quiz—Best Place offers an entertaining quiz on your preferences for retirement, and then spits out a few states it recommends based on your answers. Take it with a grain of salt; I took the quiz and answered every one of the 10 or so questions honestly—with mixed results among the three states recommended. Mississippi and Florida would not be on my personal lists of states for retirement; but the third, South Carolina, is actually where I own a vacation home and have spent a good part of my adult life.

CoMagine.org Health—Ranking of dozens of hospitals per state on different quality factors.

Insure.com—Cost of living by state and some illuminating information about the impact of insurance rates on COL.

GLORIOUS BACK NINE

Chapter Three

> *Real estate is a people game, not a house game.*
> —Todd M. Fleming

Choosing A Real Estate Pro

It is hard to get a feel for any golf community before you visit it. Few communities, for example, publish country club or homeowner association dues. Such information could cause you to decide not to pursue a community that, otherwise, seems like a good fit. When you find a golf community online that seems to match your criteria, you face perhaps one of the most important decisions of the entire process: How to qualify and engage the assistance of a local real estate professional.

How to Identify Your Real Estate Agent

When it comes to working with a local real estate agency, you have two ways to go; either work with the agency on site in the particular golf community you have targeted, if the community maintains its own real estate office; or identify an agency that knows the local golf community scene. There are benefits to both approaches, and a downside or two.

Real estate agents working for the developer or homeowner's association inside the gates of a community often sell only properties in that community. Their mission is to sell you a home inside the gates; this, on the face of it, could cause them to oversell their communities. But in 15 years, I have had zero complaints from clients about feeling pressured to buy a property or who worked with agents who bad-mouthed other communities in the area. On the contrary, real estate agents who represent a specific community tend to refrain from comparing their apples to the oranges of other local communities.

What you get when you work with an on-site agency is specialized knowledge of that community and direct answers to any questions about financial conditions, golf membership fees, activities and the overall lifestyle inside the gates. By the ethics of the real estate industry, and in most cases by law, a real estate agent is not permitted to provide fake answers to your real questions.

An independent agent not affiliated with a particular golf community can show you properties on the Multiple Listing Service (MLS) in all the local communities. They really don't care where you purchase. (But, of course, they want you to buy a home through them since they get a commission on the sale.) They are free to be more open about comparing one community to another based on your requirements and preferences. I have established a network of local professionals in most of the popular golf community areas of the Southeast; where I have not established a relationship, I interview agents on behalf of clients who ask for my assistance.

In general, the real estate professionals I work with are full-time agents who have at least 10 years experience in the local market, and have represented golf home buyers over most of that time.

Valuable Information at No Cost

I have not met a buyer's real estate agent in 15 years who charges a client a fee for representation. Their compensation is via a commission at the time of sale. That commission is typically 3% of the purchase price of the property, but can be lower if so negotiated with the seller at the time of listing. Unless you ask your agent to perform extraordinary extra services for you, you should never have to pay for their assistance.

However, buyers' agents may ask you to sign an agency agreement that ensures they earn a commission when you purchase a home with their assistance. This is only fair if they have conducted research in your behalf and toured you through multiple homes in the area. It also protects the buyer; if agents are certain they will receive a reward for their assistance, then they are likely to work even harder in their clients' behalf.

In summary, you should be confident in the professionalism and objectivity of agents both inside and outside a golf community. Just know that those inside may only be able to sell you a home located in their community. (For a list of buyer agent responsibilities, please see Appendix C.)

How long to identify a real estate agent? Either a few hours of research online or the few minutes it takes to contact me at editor@homeonthecourse.com.

GLORIOUS BACK NINE

Chapter Four

> *...a day spent with dreaming and sunsets
> and refreshing breezes cannot be bettered.*
> —Nicholas Sparks

Location = Lifestyle

The heyday for construction of golf community developments was the 1980s and '90s, although some communities, especially those in Florida, have already passed their 40th birthdays. As with human pathology, if a golf community makes it to its 40th birthday, chances are good it will be around for the long haul. And whereas such a community not only gains an edge in experience, it also tends to make fewer mistakes than do younger, unproven communities.

Commitment is Better than Involvement

Most older golf communities are run by their residents and, in many cases, the property owners are in charge of the golf club as well (often to good effect, sometimes not). Like the old story of the ham and egg breakfast—the chicken is certainly involved but the pig is really committed—communities that are run by committed residents generally are less risky than those run by a developer whose ultimate aim is to sell his lots and move on.

On balance, residents care greatly about their homes' values and, when they are in charge, they will tend to make decisions in that light. Developers care most about selling land and spec homes, and often their pricing decisions are not always in the best interests of the folks to whom they have already sold property. I have encountered a few communities, for example, in which the developer's real estate agents are compensated way less for selling lower-priced resale properties than for the developer's available dirt, creating price competition between the developer and his/her own residents inside the gates. Thankfully, this practice appears to be fading.

Vested Interests

Prospective buyers of golf community properties can protect themselves in a number of ways. Property Owner Association boards keep notes of their meetings, a good source of information about financial reserves, operations and other issues a cautious buyer will want to know. Most resident-run golf communities make their financial information available on request. I recall a conversation some years ago with the general manager at the 30-year old Champion Hills in Hendersonville, NC, who told me the country club and POA share their financial highlights with potential buyers who ask.

"...with the changing economic conditions in 2008," he said, "[clients wanted] to research and perform their due diligence carefully when considering a golf course community." In a pandemic-affected real estate market, that research is just as important today.

Champion Hills, Hendersonville, NC
Courtesy of Dave Sansom Photography

As a potential buyer in any golf community, you are within your rights to ask to see the financials; the communities are within their rights to refuse, since you are not (yet) a property owner. But the smart and stable ones won't refuse, and if they do, the strong advice here is to look elsewhere.

The same goes for inquiries about the operations and governance of golf clubs within the community. I cover this in detail in Chapter Seven and list in Appendix C some key documents you should consider reviewing.

How Safe Is Your Investment?

"Value" is a bet on the future more than a statement of current conditions. And, in that regard, some golf communities firmly in the hands of outside agencies may be even stronger than those guided solely by homeowners. Two golf communities I have watched closely—Reynolds Lake Oconee and Brunswick Forest—could not be more different in terms of property costs, size, number of golf courses and geography. However, the deep pockets owners behind Reynolds and Brunswick Forest make them contenders for risk-averse value purchasers.

Brunswick Forest is owned by the 100-year-old firm Lord Baltimore Capital, which provided the backing that made it possible for the community's excellent amenities, which include a fun and challenging golf course and an 18,000 square foot "wellness" center that was up and running shortly after land sales began. Such a strong funding resource also helped make Brunswick Forest, just 10 minutes from Wilmington, NC, one of the top-selling golf communities in the East during and immediately after the 2008 recession.

Reynolds Lake Oconee, Greensboro, GA Photo by Larry Gavrich

Reynolds Lake Oconee, though located in a remote part of central Georgia, is nevertheless large enough to provide numerous activities that help overcome its almost one-hour distance from Athens and 75 minutes from Atlanta. After original developers Mercer and Jamie Reynolds hit the skids financially, Metropolitan Life Insurance stepped in to put the Reynolds community on a more solid footing. There are few deeper pockets than Met Life's, and you cannot argue with their longtime business success and stability. Reynolds homeowners have certainly benefited: I counted only four homes for sale in early 2020 under the listed price of $400,000; yet about the time Met Life rode into town, there were a couple of dozen under the $400k mark.

Of course, as we found out during and after the 2008 recession, some developers are not abundantly resourced and many overextended themselves during an era of "cheap" money. When you visit a community not yet owned by its residents, ask tough questions about the financial resources behind it. If you are not satisfied with the answers, move on.

The contrast between the towns of Wilmington and Greensboro could not be starker; the former a thriving metropolis with a branch of the state university, the latter remotely located, an hour from a university and 90 minutes from an airport. Wilmington has a solid business climate, and Greensboro relies on its beautiful Lake Oconee and its strong attraction to retirees, as well as a new hospital and other services. Both towns will continue to attract retirees and others for the foreseeable future. However, some communities are located in towns with only one company or business, and if that business were to ever leave, the town—and those who rely on the town's services—could suffer. The advice here is to be as careful in researching a town as you are in considering the local golf community you are targeting.

Total Up All the Costs

You do not want to consider any golf communities you cannot afford. Now that seems like obvious advice, but you may look at price tags in the community and think, "Hey, we can afford that." But some of the costs in any golf community are hidden from view—until you ask the real estate agent working on your behalf.

These include the golf initiation fee which in many communities is inconsequential but, in a few, can reach beyond five figures. As mentioned earlier, the initiation fee should be part of your overall house budget. Say, for example, you have $400,000 to spend on a home and your favorite community has a private club with an initiation fee of $30,000; in that case, you will either have to revise your house budget to $370,000 or do some great negotiation on price with the seller of the home you want. (In some communities club memberships are transferable; you may be able to negotiate your way into a membership with the seller.)

Making the Numbers Work for You

Consider two homes, of similar age, with similar styles and fittings and located in two different, high-quality private golf communities. In Sample A below, you pay more for house plus golf fees initially, but your monthly dues are $3,600 less annually. In Sample B, you save a total of $20,000 up front, but your monthly outlay is $300 more. At the six-year mark, you would have saved more in dues than the $20,000 difference between the initial costs.

	Home Cost	Initiation Fees	Monthly Club HOA + Golf
Community A	$ 500,000	$5,000	$600
Community B	$ 450,000	$35,000	$900

When you are assessing your budget needs into the future, pay close attention to all carrying costs, including dues for the club membership, dues payable to the homeowner's association (and, separately, to your neighborhood association, if there is one) and property taxes. In some communities, the initiation fees will seem reasonable but the carrying costs higher than you anticipated, Some of the deluxe golf communities in Bluffton SC, just off Hilton Head Island, charge a reasonable initiation fee of around $20,000 (each offers 36 holes of splendid golf) but annual outlays for the club and homeowners' association can reach the $20,000 mark. And the club membership fees are mandatory for all property owners; more about that coming up.

Make sure you ask your real estate agent to run the numbers before you visit a specific community; otherwise you will be wasting precious time looking into a living situation you cannot afford.

Living Close to the Action

Forty years ago, land near attractive cities and towns was more plentiful, and cheaper, than it has been in the last two decades. The Landings golf community in Georgia, for example, which recently passed its 45th anniversary, is a short drive to one of the Southeast's most interesting cities, Savannah, filled with all the services Baby Boomers require and desire. And yet, once inside the gates of The Landings, you feel as if you are as far away from civilization as you are at, say, the Cliffs communities beside South Carolina's Lake Keowee, which are a good 50 minutes from Greenville, SC.

Wilmington, NC's Landfall golf community recently hit the 35-year mark, and although it is positioned on the coast, as its name suggests, and just a couple of minutes from Wrightsville Beach, it is also a mere 15 minutes from downtown Wilmington, one of the most active and growth-oriented towns on the east coast. The nearby Porters Neck Plantation golf community actually started selling lots in the early 1950s, but it did not truly reach golf community status until Tom Fazio laid out the 18-hole course that opened in 1991. Porters Neck is also 15 minutes to the center of the thriving Wilmington.

Landfall, Wilmington, NC   Photo by Larry Gavrich

The Southeast offers a nice collection of high-quality golf communities within easy reach of full-service cities with top-notch hospitals, active regional airports, entertainment options and restaurants. Those cities include Richmond, VA; Raleigh/Durham and Charlotte, NC; Greenville and Charleston, SC; Savannah and Atlanta, GA; and the major cities of Florida.

Purchase, with an Option to Rent Out

Condominium ownership was more popular 25 to 30 years ago than it is today, but as the inventories of single-family homes have dried up and prices increased nearly 10% annually before coronavirus, a comeback seemed imminent. Still, about 80% of my clients looking in the $300,000 to $400,000 range, for example, specify single-family homes rather than condos as their top choice.

Many golf resorts double as year-round or vacation golf communities. My wife's and my own vacation community, Pawleys Plantation in Pawleys Island, SC, opened in 1988 around a fine Jack Nicklaus course. We own a condo there, but those considering the community as a place to live full- or part-time can choose among patio homes—typically up to 2,000 square feet and set on ¼ acre lots—single-family homes and the aforementioned condos, some of them in townhouse style (two-stories, typically no neighbors above or below). Prices range from the low $200s for the townhouse/condos to a few big homes with marsh views for around $1 million. Pawleys Plantation shares that mix of housing options with many communities along the Carolinas coasts.

Vacation homeowners looking to defray some costs in resort communities may consider renting out their units when they are not using them. This is easier in communities with an embedded base of condos, which lend themselves to short-term rentals more than single homes do. But you can still generate income in communities largely composed of single-family homes, if their association bylaws permit renting.

DeBordieu Colony in Georgetown, SC, for example, does not present itself as a resort community, even though it includes the only beach inside a gated community on the South Carolina coast, as well as a fine Pete Dye golf course. (Note: All beaches in South Carolina are nominally public, but DeBordieu's private entrance means the public can access its beach only by boat or drop from a helicopter.) DeBordieu maintains relatively few townhomes or "villas" in its portfolio, but on DeBordieu's website, rentals get billing right along with homes for sale. For example, a three-bedroom, two-bath villa with easy access to the beach, a pool and the golf course rents for between $1,700 and $3,400 per week, depending on season. The owners are likely paying a fee of at least 40% for DeBordieu Realty to handle all aspects of the rental, including marketing, housekeeping and insurance. But for a couple looking for a few weeks a year by the beach and an excellent golf course to play when they are in residence, as well as a way to help pay for it, the numbers may work to their advantage.

I explore the rent vs. not rent decision in Chapter Nine.

DeBordieu Colony clubhouse, Georgetown, SC Photo by Larry Gavrich

Acting Your Age...Or Not

Some golf communities choose to keep young people—as in younger than 55—from from owning property. Most age-restricted communities require that at least one spouse or partner be older than 55. But the reality is that most golf communities in the Southeast, by the nature of their locations or the cost of real estate, comprise a large percentage of retirees, whether officially age-restricted or not.

Rural golf communities are generally the most reliably populated with seniors because of a lack of job-attracting industry nearby and, therefore, a smaller population of families and children in the area. But even in the more populated coastal towns in and around Myrtle Beach, for example, which has a thriving tourism industry, young parents are just starting to build their careers and family lives and do not have the financial resources to pay the comparably higher prices in an organized community, nor the fees to join the golf club. Residents of most of the dozens of golf communities in the Myrtle Beach area rarely see a school bus come through the gates or hear the squeals of toddlers splashing in the community's pool (except, perhaps, during summers when grandma and grandpa have visitors).

In short, you can satisfy your need to be around mature adults even without signing up for the restrictions of a 55+ community. And those energized by being around young people should target golf communities near urban areas that attract upwardly mobile careerists and families.

Chances are that during that initial "kitchen table" discussion, you agreed on whether you wanted to live with people your age or with a range of age groups, and whether you wanted the peace and quiet of a remote location or the activities typical of a near-urban area. Therefore, the final decision on the demographics of your new community should not take more than a few minutes.

Note: In Appendix A at the back of the book, we list dozens of golf communities, the vast majority of which I have visited.

GLORIOUS BACK NINE

Chapter Five

> *Don't play too much golf. Two rounds a day are plenty.*
> —Harry Vardon

Choosing the Golf Course(s)

Extra Golf Courses Add Variety...and Cost

If you have been pointing toward a retirement that includes golf on many courses within a small geographic area, look no farther than the Southeast where you will find as many as 10 golf courses to play under one membership. Over the years, for example, the famed Pinehurst Resort has built and stitched together a portfolio of 10 area courses into one membership. You will share the fairways with transient golfers on vacation, but with a total of 10, one is always available for member play only. Initiation fees are less than $50,000 for access to all of them, and the only limitation is that you must own a property in one of the communities adjacent to a Pinehurst-affiliated course.

There is a wide range of multi-course communities across the Southeast. The Cliffs communities, for example, offer its member residents a choice of seven beautifully groomed layouts across the upstate and lake regions of South Carolina, as well as one a half hour from Asheville, NC. Initiation fees are $50,000. Some of the courses are as far as an hour from each other and, as you might expect, members tend to play most of their golf at their home courses. At The Landings in Savannah, members have six excellent layouts available on its 4,800 acres for just a $30,000 initiation fee. The courses range in style from parkland to marshland with varying degrees of difficulty.

The six fine courses at Reynolds Lake Oconee in northern Georgia, like those at The Landings, are within a few minutes of each other and carry similar architectural pedigrees, with designs by Jack Nicklaus, Fazio, Rees Jones and others. Reynolds' initiation fee depends on which courses the member decides to join; the costs start in the $20,000 range and run up to near $70,000, with dues rising appreciably as the number of courses rises. With the exception of some play by guests of the on-site Ritz Carlton, Reynolds courses are private.

Some golfers prefer to get to know a golf course or two intimately well and find the nuances of 18 or 36 hole layouts more interesting than a greater abundance of golf courses. They also find the monthly costs more reasonable since maintenance of one course is less costly than maintenance of multiple layouts.

Access to Hundreds of Other Courses

During and after the 2008 recession, many private and semi-private clubs decided to turn over management to third parties. The most well-known of these are ClubCorp and Troon. Typically, for an extra bump-up in monthly dues payment, these mega-golf club operators open up their nationwide roster of clubs to members of the clubs they manage. For example, if you are a member of the Woodside Plantation Country Club in Aiken, SC, which is managed by ClubCorp, and you are traveling, say, to the Phoenix/Scottsdale area, you can arrange to play golf

CHOOSING THE GOLF COURSE(S)

at one of the five ClubCorp-managed clubs in the area. ClubCorp and Troon, through its similarly styled membership, also offer access to social clubs, discounts for travel and many other services.

Carting Yourself Around

As we age, most of us are forced to use a golf cart to negotiate the four miles or so that comprise most 18-hole golf courses. Some golf community clubs provide the option of using your own golf cart on the course and charge an annual "trail fee" for the privilege. A used golf cart will cost an average of $5,300, a new one in the $9,000 range (although you can easily spend up to $20,000 for all the bells and whistles). Couples for whom this seems like an attractive deal will have to run the numbers carefully. Such trail fees can run to as much as $2,000 a year and more. If the club charges, say, $30 to rent a cart for each round, you'll need to play at least 65 rounds during the year to make the investment work...

...unless the golf community permits the use of golf carts on its streets as well as its golf course. In that case, the return on investment in the cart includes the ease with which you can visit friends, and travel back and forth to the golf course, the pools and the clubhouse. I will never forget the morning I approached in my rental car one of the six golf clubs at The Landings in Savannah to make my 8:30 a.m. shotgun start. As I drove over a rise in the road just before the club entrance, a dozen golf carts in a sort of formation appeared headed toward me, reminiscent of the famous scene of the helicopters coming over the horizon in the movie *Apocalypse Now*.

If you have your eye on a golf community that permits carts and is larger than, say, 1,000 acres, consider the investment. Our vacation home is in a golf-cart-friendly community, and although I cannot justify the expense as a part-time resident, I feel a bit jealous when I see friends heading for the golf course in their carts.

On Course for Growing Old

At 60 or 65, you might be busting the ball 225 yards or farther, but five or 10 years from now, age may catch up with your golf game. In that case, you may need to switch from a layout that plays a total of, say, 6,500 yards to one that plays under 6,000. Therefore, whether you are considering a golf community with one course or more, you will need to ensure that the layout will be appropriately challenging and fun for you later on. Check out the course scorecard for not only overall length, but also focus on the par 4s to make sure that, from the tee box you will likely play in the future, you won't be hitting fairway metal second shots on most of them. Ditto any forced carries that will require you to hit long shots over menacing bodies of water; that may be easy today but down the road, long carries could kill your enjoyment of the game.

Of course, when you visit a community that you are serious about, make sure to play the golf course—or courses—at least a couple of times each, and pay attention to the tee boxes. If you find the course either overly challenging or too easy, move up or back one or two tee boxes on the second day of play to adjust the degree of difficulty.

Ladies should pay particular attention to whether the course from the women's tees produces many forced carries or long approach shots.

Chapter Six

> *Now and then it is good to pause
> in the pursuit of happiness and just be happy*
> — Guillaume Appolonaire

The Essence Of A Community

Now to plan your visits. Any community proud of itself should be happy to show off its goods to prospective buyers. Most high-quality communities make it easy and financially reasonable to check them out through what are ubiquitously known as "Discovery Packages." Typically three days and two nights in duration, you pay a reasonable fee (from $149 to $400) to essentially become a member for a few days. That gives you access to the clubhouse, the golf course and other amenities, and overnight accommodations, most often on the property. In some cases, where rental inventories are small or non-existent, the community will offer lodging in a local hotel or bed and breakfast.

Of course, the community's real estate office will expect you to spend a couple of hours with them on a tour of the community and, if you want, a look at a few houses in your price range. The house visits are purely discretionary at this point, and if you have arranged to visit other communities in the area, I recommend deferring a look inside any houses until you decide which community or two you like best. Finding a house you like in a community that is not your first choice will only cause confusion. And unless you need to buy a house right away, other homes will come on the market in the community you prefer well before decision time. Chances are good that house will suit you just fine.

The Likability Factor

I am often asked by clients, "How will we know if the people in a community will like us...or we will like them?" I always feel tempted to respond, "Well, how likable are you?" but the more politic answer is to suggest taking advantage of a discovery package. The on-site real estate agency or the membership director will arrange for you to play golf with other members, eat in the clubhouse with residents and engage in other activities as you see fit. Most golf communities that offer discovery packages have "ambassador" programs that assign a resident couple to socialize, play golf and dine with you and introduce you to other residents, as well as answer all the questions you care to ask. By the end of a couple or three days, you will know how you fit in and what your future neighbors are like.

In truth, I have never heard a couple say that people in the community they moved to were difficult to live with. Do they have different attitudes about politics and social mores? Yes, but likely so do your neighbors down the street where you live now. You'll manage, and so will your new neighbors.

One other thing to keep the anxiety level about relocation to a minimum: Most communities in the South are composed of residents from somewhere else, many of whom once had the exact same anxieties you may have about blending in. Recalling those feelings, they will be sympathetic and will do what they can to make you feel comfortable, not only during your "discovery" phase but

THE ESSENCE OF A COMMUNITY

after you move in. And keep in mind that a healthy real estate market in their community, one in which homes do not stay on the market for too long, stabilizes the value of their own homes. They want you to join them...and stay.

A Few Key Questions to Ask During Your Visit

Over the course of a visit to a golf community you have targeted, you will ask a whole bunch of questions. (If not, you have wasted an opportunity.) Below are a few that you should definitely address (others will come to you during the visit):

What are the amounts of the financial reserves for the HOA and country club?

Every organization must maintain a "rainy day fund" for unplanned events. For golf communities, these include hurricanes, clubhouse fires, mudslides and numerous other acts of God. You hope these never happen but, if they do, you want to know that your community has enough in the bank to get by. Well-run clubs and communities keep at least 6 months worth of expenses in reserve, many of them a year's worth or more.

Who owns/runs the golf club?

Just because a developer built a golf club 30 years ago to attract homebuyers doesn't mean that developer, or those who bought the club in later years, are compelled legally to keep it as a golf course—unless the original covenants indicate it will always be a golf course. If the members of the club who live inside the gates of the community purchased the club from the developer years ago, then they are responsible for keeping the club sustainable; only a vote of members could give up that right. This rarely happens since members understand that the value of their real estate is tied to the quality of the community's golf course(s). In short, ask to see the original covenants governing the golf course, especially if the developer or a non-resident group owns the club.

What is the status and potential for member assessments?

Some golf clubs that suffered during the 2008 recession found it necessary to ask their members to help sustain the club financially through extra assessments, above and beyond normal dues payments. Other communities are coming to an age at which the golf course, especially greens, clubhouse and other amenities, require renovations or a complete redo. The Landings outside Savannah, for example, which passed its 45th anniversary recently, is replacing one of its three clubhouses and renovating other facilities in the next few years, for which they have asked their residents for either a one-time lump sum contribution or an assessment added to their monthly dues for the next 10 years.

These assessments are not developed frivolously but typically have the buy-in of the majority of residents. You should not be intimidated by the prospect of assessments, but you should be aware of what might be on the horizon. On the other hand, if you fall in love with a community that has made the improvements in recent years and is done charging its residents for the updating, good for you—your timing was impeccable.

Are the important services I require close by?

It is generally true that real estate prices in golf communities are inversely proportional to their distances from thriving urban communities. Upscale communities like The Reserve at Lake Keowee and most of The Cliffs communities in the Carolina high country are exceptions because they are loaded with deluxe amenities. You can purchase a nice lakefront home in a community like Savannah Lakes Village or Keowee Key in rural South Carolina for a very reasonable price, but if you covet nearby shopping or a selection of excellent restaurants within a half hour, consider communities closer to Greenville, Charleston or other fair-sized cities. The same goes for those people with health issues who require good doctors and a hospital within a half hour. Assess your lifestyle requirements carefully and then do the research to determine whether the requirements of that lifestyle will be within reach.

How Does the HOA or Developer Market the Community?

Real estate values are directly related to the marketing of a golf community. If a developer still runs the community you are looking at, ask about the annual marketing budget and how it is spent. If the developer is no longer in charge, ask if the residents (HOA) have the authority to market the community without restrictions. Many high-quality golf communities in the Southeast endured months of disruption after their developers left. Understand also that a golf community's marketing budget is figured into the sales price of new homes, which can inflate the costs of homesites.

Reserve at Lake Keowee, Sunset, SC. Photo by Larry Gavrich

Getting Bugged

This may seem trivial, but I have personal experience with the issue of annoying bugs in the Southeast. Some members of my family are reluctant to re-visit us at our Pawleys Island, SC, vacation home because, during a family reunion there in 2001, mosquitoes were a problem. As bad timing would have it, that was the only time in the 19 years we have owned our condo that the bugs were such a bother. A spraying program (non-toxic, all natural) throughout the year has done an excellent—and quiet—job of tamping down the problem (although, in truth, going for a walk at dusk can be an issue). Bugs are ubiquitous in the Southeast, especially in low-lying areas, and it is a good idea to ask the locals about any bug problems and to ask the leaders of the HOA in the community you are visiting how they address the issue.

The South is home to all kinds of critters that some who migrate there may not have met outside a zoo. These include alligators, the occasional wild pig (boar) and a number of exotic snakes, some harmless, some poisonous. In almost all cases, they do not bother you if you do not bother them.

On these initial exploratory visits, a couple of hours at each community should do the trick, unless you take advantage of a discovery package and stay for a couple or three days. Even then, you are not a prisoner of that community and can go off site and visit a few other communities in the area. To do a proper job of scouting a particular area, count on two or three days. If you have a week to explore, head off to another area and its golf communities before heading back home.

Chapter Seven

Fitting in is about assessing a situation and becoming who you need to be in order to be accepted. Belonging, on the other hand, doesn't require us to change who we are; it requires us to be who we are.
— Brene Brown

To Belong Or Not Belong

There are both tangible and intangible reasons for paying comparably higher initiation fees and dues to join a private club inside the community you choose (or, in some cases, just down the road). I count among the tangible reasons:

- The generally better maintenance of the golf course
- The ability to get to know your fellow members more quickly than you would at a course with a lot of outside play
- The quality of the club's staff (assuming an experienced and involved golf professional, general manager and board)
- At least in theory, the greater respect shown to the golf course by members who have a vested interest in conditions. (Many transient golfers at public and

resort courses do not repair ball marks, replace divots or otherwise show proper respect for someone else's golf course.)

Intangible Reason to Join the Club

The intangible reason for joining a private club is the way you will be treated compared with a public club. For example, I can't put a price on it, but I like it when the guys at the bag drop say, "Hey Mr. Gavrich, good to see you back at Pawleys Plantation." Pawleys Plantation is actually a semi-private club with lots of play by vacationing golfers; at peak times, members can make advanced tee-time reservations but, occasionally, I have not been able to get out on the same day I call. Still, I like the whiff of a private club atmosphere at semi-private club prices, and the added revenue generated by transient golfers helps maintain my part-time course.

Most couples considering a move to a golf community are golfers or those non-golfers who enjoy looking at landscaped green spaces. All those considering golf community living—golfers or not—need to make sure that the golf club inside the gates is successful and, for sure, sustainable. A failing country club almost always leads to falling home values. A successful one props up property values.

Although golf memberships fall into only two broad categories—private and semi-private—there are permutations within each that make the appropriate choice mesmerizingly confusing. (Some notes on public course options later in this chapter.)

Pawleys Plantation, Pawleys Island, SC Photo by Larry Gavrich

Equity vs Non-Equity Memberships

    The plain vanilla non-equity option is the most popular type of private club membership and has served folks well since golf clubs became private domains in the early 20th Century. Indeed, the straight-up payment of an initiation fee, with no promise of any of it being returned at a later date, saved many people a considerable amount of money in the wake of the 2008 recession. Non-equity members who were pressed for discretionary cash during the recession were able to just walk away from their memberships without losing an appreciably larger "down payment," or giving up on the promise of a refund.

    Members who signed up for comparatively pricey equity memberships that promised a full or partial refund after resignation from their clubs are still waiting for their money more than a decade later. Clubs that once touted the glories of such "nothing to lose" plans have dropped them like the hot potatoes they were. The few that remain generally pay back their "depositors" on a four-to-one basis; for every four new members, one former member gets the deposit back. Lotsa luck with that.

There are, however, some "equity" memberships that can make sense for couples who expect to enjoy many years in one golf community. These are the equity memberships with non-refundable initiation fees. The "equity" ensures that if the club were ever dissolved, each then-current member would receive an equal percentage of what is left over after all debts are paid. Equity members typically also get a vote on the major club decisions and also share the benefits of capital reserves built by those non-refundable initiation fees. Such equity memberships can make a lot of sense for those couples who plan to remain members over a decade or more.

It is undeniable that, in the wake of the recession, non-equity private clubs lost members, in some cases lots of members. And that exerted pressures on revenue and, in turn, on maintenance of the golf courses and related amenities. Some private courses had no choice but to open play to the public to generate much needed revenue. Some of those clubs got used to that revenue and, today, remain private in name only. Others fell so far behind that their courses became unsustainable; they have since been turned over to developers for additional housing, where the community's covenants and the local courts permit. For example, in 2019, after much protest by homeowners adjacent to the Indian Wells Golf Club in the Myrtle Beach area, the local court approved developer plans to build new houses on the former course.

But many fine non-equity clubs continue, and they are the proper choice for those couples content with modest financial outlays and the security that comes with no penalties if you simply walk away.

Which Clubs are Safest

A club can be owned by one of three parties—its members, the developer of the community or a third-party owner. In general, but not always, a member-owned club is the most secure. Members run the club through a board they elect, and with committees that, in the ideal situation, include a wide range of members. The best boards are those comprising members across a range of ages and backgrounds, as well as those that don't appoint chairpersons simply because they have the loudest voices. Those who may have led a business firm during their careers or a small family business may have the skills but often not the spirit of comity needed to run a country club board. Many are used to having their own way, and that can be the ruination of a country club board.

You can mitigate potential surprises as a future club member with some due diligence about club governance. When you visit the community you believe is right for you, ask to speak with a member of the club's board. Ask about term limits for board members, whether there is turnover or multi-year terms that might imply a "good old boys" club. It might also be a good idea to get your hands on the board members' resumes to see if the diversity among them meets your expectations.

Then too, especially in communities with older residents, age can have a negative effect on investments in the club. Older members who may be using club facilities less as they age may be inclined to vote against improvements. If you are considering a community composed mostly of retirees, inquire about the composition of the club board and whether dues levels drop at a certain age. Such a dues plan could limit friction between the oldest residents and others.

Deep-Pocketed Developers Imply Security

Although any private golf club can hit the rocks for any number of reasons, the most risky are those owned by either the developer of the community or a third party. Unlike a member-owned club whose board has a responsibility to its fellow members and residents, a developer has no such responsibility unless the original covenants at the time of initial development are strictly written. In many cases, those agreements stipulate that once sales of properties have reached a specific level—75 percent of the total in the community is not unusual—the club is offered for sale (or turnover) to members at a pre-arranged price. In many agreements, the developer will have the right to sell to a third party if the residents do not opt to purchase at the originally agreed price. Also, ask if there are deed restrictions on the property on which the golf course is built. In some cases, use of the property will be for recreational purposes only, such as golf or, potentially, hiking or parkland. In other cases, no restrictions on use could mean homes might be built there in the future.

Some developers do a great job of managing the country club, but prospective members need to keep one important thing in mind: Input from members about the running of the club is discretionary on the part of the developer or third-party owner. They will likely form an advisory committee of members to provide input, but the developer may or may not consider that input when making decisions, especially at times of financial stress.

Mandatory Memberships Make Scary Sense

There is one type of private club membership that, on the surface, seems as perilous as the defunct refundable equity membership. Typically referred to as "bundled" memberships, some communities choose to require that all residents join the community's country club. National builder Lennar bundles golf membership in some of its golf communities, but the costs are relatively nominal.

TO BELONG OR NOT BELONG

Some upscale communities attach membership to every property and compel new property owners to sign up for a club membership from day one. The reasoning, from the community's standpoint, is simple: If all homeowners pay their monthly dues, then the golf course, clubhouse and other amenities will always have the funds required to remain in tip-top condition.

This means, of course, that all residents who want or need to sell their homes someday will have to do so to a buyer willing to become a member of the club. This presents no problem when the economy is in good shape, but in times of recession, such as after 2008, resale potentials can dry up as people conserve their discretionary cash. And if you believe that enthusiasm for playing golf is on the wane among retirees—I have not seen compelling evidence of this although the media enjoys writing about it—then you may want to go the conservative route and avoid such obligations.

But if you crave a high-quality golf club and are willing to take on a bit of risk in order to play on some of the best golf courses in any golf communities, mandatory makes sense. At Colleton River Club in Bluffton, SC, for example, which features two of the best golf courses inside the gates of any coastal community, the joining fees for the club and its Jack Nicklaus and Pete Dye golf courses is relatively modest at around $20,000. But in order to keep the golf courses in pristine condition and the clubhouses at a standard members expect, carrying costs in the community, more than half of it club dues, are nearly $20,000 per year, as they are at neighboring communities Belfair and Berkeley Hall (36 holes of Tom Fazio golf at each).

Colleton River Club, Bluffton, SC

Those financial obligations are why during the recession of 2008 and in the wake of the COVID-19 economy, some perfectly nice lots that in the mid-2000s sold for as much as $400,000, were listed for just $1!

Cliffs Dwellers' Revised Plan

One of the most controversially creative forms of club membership was deployed by The Cliffs communities from the late 1990s up to the 2008 recession. Its vaunted full-golf membership program, which included access to world-class wellness centers and a wide range of other deluxe amenities, assessed an initiation fee as high as $125,000.

Technically, membership in the Cliffs clubs was "voluntary," but membership was attached to the homesites that Cliffs owners purchased from the developer. If you didn't sign up for golf membership at closing, then you could never upgrade to that level of membership, and you couldn't sell your home to someone who wanted a golf membership. In short, there was no customer flexibility in the program, and you were stuck with the decision you made at closing. This was fine during the roaring 90s and early 2000s, but when the 2008 recession hit, sales plummeted; no new buyers were going to sign up for such an obligation, and it was too late for original developer Jim Anthony to consider modifications to his membership program. Anthony departed and The Cliffs was on the ropes.

Today, under the ownership of South Street Partners, which also runs the Kiawah Island operations, The Cliffs communities offer a much more flexible approach to membership than before. You must still commit to some kind of membership when you buy a property or home at The Cliffs, but that membership—at a much more reasonable $50,000 initiation fee—can be either upgraded or downgraded over time, depending on circumstances. In other words, just because you hit an age when you can't play golf anymore doesn't mean you need to move to another community or continue paying for something you don't use.

Woodside, in the popular and charming town of Aiken, SC, maintains a membership plan that seems especially reasonable, given the twin objectives of sustaining the on-site private country club and its 36 holes of golf, and providing flexibility to members at a reasonable cost. Social membership is priced at $2,500 and an additional $7,500 to upgrade to full-family golf membership. Golf dues are $525 per month per couple and include any children under the age of 23.

Woodside, Aiken, SC   Photo by Larry Gavrich

Getting to Know the Club Before You Join

You can learn a lot about a golf community's club and its activities from its web site, but not everything. Steve Benz, a subscriber to my newsletter, *Home On The Course*, shared with me a technique he used when he and his wife were considering different options for golf communities.

"I asked the club's membership director for a year's worth of their club newsletter," Steve told me. "They provided good data on the club's culture, events and priorities."

Most clubs publish a newsletter for members, and occasionally you will find them posted online. These will often include calendars of events, but they also share details about the events themselves, with accompanying photos of participants. Review enough of these communications and, as Steve did, you will get a feel for how the club operates in behalf of its members.

One other approach you could take is to time your visit to a community for the days its men's and women's golf groups play and, through your sales agent, get invited to participate. (You might be asked to throw a few dollars into the pot for the day's event, but it is a small price to pay for the knowledge you will gain by playing with your future fellow-residents. And, who knows, you might win a few bucks.)

The Public Option

Although a private club membership may speed a couple's integration into the social life of a golf community, there are myriad other ways to do that through clubhouse events (for which only a lower-priced social membership will be necessary), other activities (pool, fitness center, social clubs) and just the old-fashioned neighborly way of stopping to chat with fellow residents when you are out for a walk. If you intend to play golf only a couple of days a week or less, a private club with the dues to match may not be financially appropriate. Make an assessment of the public golf courses in the area you have targeted and play an inspection round or two at each. If they suit your game and your pocketbook, you have found a viable alternative to an expensive club membership.

In recent years, groups of retirees, some who live in private golf communities, have dropped their memberships and organized a constant string of outings at local public courses. They save money and get to play a variety of layouts.

In many areas, especially in the wake of the recession, public courses have been gobbled up and merged into low-cost, multi-course memberships. Spend a couple hundred dollars a year, and you can play, for example, 22 local courses in the Myrtle Beach area at deeply discounted prices.

Caledonia Golf & Fish Club, Pawleys Island, SC. Photo by Larry Gavrich

It is easy to figure out if the public option is the right one for you. Take whatever the annual fee is for membership, divide by 12 for your monthly dues equivalent, then estimate how often you will play each month, multiply that by the discounted green fee, add it to the monthly dues and you can pretty much figure out your total monthly costs and the true cost per round.

Use the same math for private club membership. Divide the monthly dues by the number of rounds you expect to play and, voila, you have a cost per round. Don't forget, though, you have to consider any initiation fee you paid and amortize that over the number of years you expect to belong to the club. Also, keep in mind that many public golf courses bundle their cart fees into the overall green fee. At a private club, you will pay for the use of the golf cart each time you play, unless your club permits use of your own golf cart in exchange for an annual "trail fee" payment.

And you thought keeping score in golf was easy.

Chapter Eight

> *Travel and change of place impart new vigor to the mind.*
> — Seneca

Perhaps Start With A Vacation Home

If you can afford it, there is no better way to get to know a golf community than by first buying and using a vacation home there. Over at least a few weeks every year, you get to know your neighbors, the golf course and the subtleties of life inside the gates.

Resort Areas Good for Rentals

That is what happened when my wife, children and I began vacationing on the South Carolina coast in the 1990s. In the latter part of the decade, we returned from our Connecticut home a couple of years in a row to Pawleys Plantation in Pawleys Island, SC. There was something for everyone there; golf for my son and me, a beautiful ocean beach for my wife and daughter five minutes away, and plenty of friendly neighbors, many of whom lived there year-round. Some homeowners looking to defray costs rent out their units when they are not using them. This is easier in communities with an embedded base of condos, which lend themselves to short-term rentals more than single homes do.

To Rent Out or Not

Yet those looking for a vacation home in a golf community face a major decision, which is whether to rent it out when they are not using it, or to keep it available for family, friends and last-minute decisions to fly or drive there for a long weekend. If you choose to forgo renting out your home, you will have the freedom to keep clothing in the closets for last minute trips and the security that your furniture will not be treated poorly by short-term renters. My wife and I chose not to rent out our vacation home.

The financial aspects of renting out your vacation home are complicated. Here are a couple of major considerations in deciding whether to become a vacation landlord or not:

- Is your main purpose in purchasing a vacation home to have a place that family and friends can use whenever they want? Or is it to generate income that will defray costs in anticipation of the home appreciating over the years?
- Will you use your vacation home for fewer than 14 days or more than 14 days in a calendar year? Fewer than 14 days and the home can be treated as a business for tax purposes; more than 14 and it will be a considered a personal residence.
- Will you hire a local real estate management company to handle marketing of your home, bookings, cleanup after the guests depart and organizing repairs if necessary? Or will you be able to use VRBO or AirBnB as your booking agent? Either way, you will pay a healthy percentage of your rental revenue.
- Keep in mind that whether you use your vacation home for business or pleasure, there will be expenses

that include homeowner association dues, country club dues, unplanned repairs and, of course, property tax (in addition to any management fee you might pay to agencies who handle bookings and maintenance).

If you intend to use your vacation home for most of a peak season—say a winter in Florida—why go through the hassles of being a landlord for the months when many people won't be interested in visiting (e.g. summers), and when your rental income will likely not cover your costs?

Whatever you decide to do, the strong advice here is to engage a tax accountant or to do enough research to understand the particulars about renting out a second home. Only then should you feel comfortable that you know what you are getting into.

Dual-Season Resort Areas are Best for Rentals

Some locations that are magnets for vacation homeowners have dual peak seasons and afford those wishing to both use and rent out their homes an opportunity to have the best of both situations. Consider the Myrtle Beach area, for example. The months of February through May and September through November tend to be popular with golfers from the northern U.S. and Canada who are looking for a jump on the golf season in early spring or an extension of the summer season in the late fall. The summer months in the Myrtle Beach area, however, tend to be a magnet for beach-going families for whom golf may only be an occasional activity. If you intend to use your vacation home near the beach in a place like Myrtle Beach for just a few weeks a year, the rental income potential will generally be positive.

Contrast that with Florida. Northerners have plenty of warm weather June through August, and a Florida vacation is not their top of mind in summer (except, perhaps, for Disney World with their school-age kids). Rental properties in the Sunshine State that are fully booked in the winter months tend to stand idle during summer. A couple who owns a winter home in Florida is not likely to find renters for the summer unless they own a home just outside the gates to Disney World.

Two-Home Solution

There is one way to get around the Florida heat in summer and the brutal winters in, say, New England: Maintain homes in both places and jump back and forth when the weather, and the spirit, moves you. This can also help get retired couples over the angst of moving away for more than half a year from children and grandchildren who live in the North. For many grandparents, current and future, family exerts a stronger pull than does a warm climate and year-round golf; they decide not to relocate, either staying put or downsizing from their primary homes and moving into smaller homes or condos nearby.

But it may not have to be that way.

One couple I know, for example, had spent 15 years from October to April at Willoughby Country Club in Stuart, FL, before returning for the summer to a Connecticut condo that is not in a golf community. (During summer, Ed played occasional golf on public courses within 20 minutes or so of their condo.) Their three sons and grandchildren all live within two hours of their Connecticut home, two of the families within a half hour. It all had worked out well for them before they sold their Florida home a year ago.

My guess is that the two-home solution (in 2020) requires about $600,000 to spend on the two homes, split in whichever way it makes sense. Some rural golf communities in the South offer homes in the mid $200s range that will be suitable for many, leaving about $350,000 for a home up North. The wild cards for many who consider owning two homes in retirement are the extra carrying costs—taxes, monthly club dues, homeowner association fees. But these can be overcome, for example, by finding a nice home in the North that is not in a golf community but, rather, close to good daily-fee golf. That way you avoid both the golf membership and homeowner dues.

PERHAPS START WITH A VACATION HOME

There are literally thousands of combinations for you to consider.

The Option of Condo Ownership

Condominiums are ideal for vacation ownership, with no lawns or landscaping for the homeowner to worry about and a size that is most appropriate for part-time residency. Having neighbors close by is generally a blessing in that they can keep an eye on your condo while you are hundreds of miles away back home. Our next door neighbor in Pawleys Island, SC, has entered our condo, at our request, after severe thunderstorms to check for leaks or power outages. Of course, having neighbors on the other side of a wall means, in some cases, you might hear a dog barking, occasional loud music and other noises.

Condo ownership demands even more tough questions than for a single home. Focus especially on financial reserves held by the condo's association to cover planned and unexpected expenses. Condo associations have a tendency to under-reserve for such expenses in order to attract prospective buyers with the lowest possible association fees (dues). That can often be a fool's paradise, especially after a hurricane blows through and trees fall down on people's homes. A condo association is responsible for all exteriors and landscaping, and that means the costs to not only remove the trees but to repair the damage to your neighbor's—or your—home is borne by the association and its members (and, you hope, the association's insurance carrier).

Exchange Your Home, See the World

For globe-trotting couples or those who want to be, a vacation home offers another impressive benefit—a house exchange opportunity, an arrangement in which you swap a stay at your home for the use of someone else's home, cost-free, at hundreds of locations in the U.S. and around the world. My wife and I have done it, and the experience led us to establish a deep friendship with the Scottish couple with whom we exchanged homes.

Thanks to a home exchange, my first trip to the Scottish coast on the North Sea and the beautiful village of Crail was without a fee for lodging.

Although you might be reluctant to swap your primary home, a vacation home provides you extra flexibility in terms of timing your exchange. However, make sure that the property owner's association in your community permits "short-term" stays; in 2019, in our own neighborhood condo association, our fellow residents voted to disallow any rentals or exchanges of less than one year's duration. We voted against it.

Chapter Nine

The universe is wider than our views of it.
— Henry David Thoreau

A View To A Thrill

The hierarchy of the most desirable views in golf communities is consistent, no matter the geography. At the top is water, and the most treasured water view is of the ocean. Without the ocean, inland golf communities command their highest prices for long lake views and, if the community is at some altitude, long-range mountain views. Somewhere in the middle of the hierarchy of prices are lots facing the golf course, whose typical values are around half those of the water views and generally on the order of 20% to 30% more than prices for wooded lots. Those wooded lots may be the least prized but they do afford many people the opportunity to buy into a golf community that might otherwise be a stretch for them. And once in place, you can always walk or bicycle to the water. Moreover, if you make friends easily, you might wangle an invitation to one of those multi-million dollar homes with a killer view. Chances are their owners didn't pay the high price just to enjoy the view by themselves.

Real estate, of course, is valued on three basic principles: Location, Location, Location. Golf community developers and real estate experts know precisely which features are most desired by buyers, and at or near the top of the list are views.

What You See is What You Pay For

Most golf communities in the Southeast feature at least some body of water inside their boundaries. Inland, it is typically a lake or river. On the coast, it is the ocean, the marshland of the Low Country, or perhaps a river. In the western sections of the Carolinas, eastern Tennessee and upstate Georgia, the dominant topography is mountains, sometimes with a lake but often not. It is rare to find a golf community lacking any of these topographical features; the most famous of those is probably the Sandhills area of North Carolina, home to Pinehurst.

Water views in any developed community, with or without a golf course, command the highest prices of any natural features, and by a large factor. Few of us would turn down a commanding water view if money were no object. But some water view lots and homes are priced on a par with a Fifth Avenue Manhattan apartment. For example, in a private golf community like DeBordieu Colony in Georgetown, SC, 40 minutes south of Myrtle Beach, the most expensive home in the community, with 7 bedrooms and 7 ½ baths, faces the ocean and was priced in August 2020 at $2.85 million. The lowest priced home in DeBordieu in August 2020 was listed for $760,000.

Float Your Boat...or Canoe

But for those who long for a commanding water view, there are some relative bargains to be had. One golf community in North Carolina that impressed me with its fair real estate prices and water orientation is Cypress Landing, located in the tongue-twisting town of Chocowinity. Much of Cypress Landing runs beside the westernmost extension of the Pamlico River, which flows directly in from the Atlantic Ocean; and although its fun-to-play golf course keeps its distance, the Pamlico is very much in view. When I checked in mid-2020, I found one 4-bedroom, 3-bath home with a view of the Chocowinity Bay listed for just $439,000.

Cypress Landing is just 20 minutes from Greenville, NC, which is home to East Carolina University and one of the largest medical centers in the Southeast. The golf community feels remote but is proximate to important services.

Cypress Landing, Chocowinity, NC   Photo by Larry Gavrich

If you don't mind the more placid nature of lake views (no waves), you will pay a lot less for them than for ocean views, sometimes dramatically so, but still enjoy expansive views of water. The 35-year-old golf community of Keowee Key in Salem, SC, demonstrates that waterfront properties are not just for the ultra-wealthy. Located on Lake Keowee in rural South Carolina, about 20 minutes from Clemson University, the difference between lots on the waterfront at Keowee Key and "interior" lots is significant, according to local real estate data. But the waterfront lots are about as low-priced as you will find in any quality golf community. When I checked listings at Keowee Key in August 2020, I found nicely sized waterfront lots for sale as low as $60,000, compared with a lot with excellent views of the golf course priced at $6,500. The lowest priced home I found with a view of the lake was listed at $525,000, with 3 bedrooms and 2 baths on 1 ¼ acres.

Savannah Lakes Village in rural McCormick, SC, features even more-reasonably priced lots that face directly onto Lake Thurmond. In August 2020, I found one waterfront lot, just under a half acre in size, priced at just $10,000. The lowest priced home I found with a lake view was $199,000.

Savannah Lakes Village, McCormick, SC   Photo by Larry Gavrich

Developers take advantage of the wild differences in perceived values, and they price their water-view lots accordingly, especially in higher-end, well-established golf communities. The deluxe community Reserve at Lake Keowee, a short drive from Keowee Key, features the same number of golf holes as does Keowee Key and half those of Savannah Lakes; waterfront lots there begin around $100,000. The Reserve's golf course, designed by Jack Nicklaus, is excellent, and its comfortable hilltop and expansive rustic clubhouse mirrors the community's other deluxe amenities. It stands to reason that its real estate would be priced comparably higher.

Cliffs at Keowee Vineyards, Sunset, SC   Photo by Larry Gavrich

Marsh Ado About Nothing

Most of my clients prefer coastal locations to inland ones. In the Low Country of the Carolinas, "coastal" means mostly marshland. Yet many who prefer water views don't consider marshland "water," although at high tide the marsh can resemble a large lake with reeds growing out of it. And at certain times of the year and under certain sunlight conditions, those reeds become beautiful heather-colored fields of wheat or large verdant meadows. (You can tell from my rhapsodic prose that I am afflicted with marsh fever.)

The problem for some is that, at low tide, the marsh resembles a mud swamp. Locals refer to it as "pluff (plough) mud," and Charleston magazine once described it as "the mother sauce of all things Low Country." If you can't love, or learn to love, the sauce—yes, there are unique smells associated with it, but nothing an oyster lover can't get used to—then our advice is to steer clear of the area of the coast from north of Myrtle Beach south to Georgia. Otherwise, it is as close as you will get to the ocean for less than seven figures. And at high tide, you can float your boat in the marsh, albeit a canoe or other small craft.

Bargain marsh views have become rare in recent years as those who cannot afford ultra-pricy oceanfront properties, but want to live near the ocean, have opted for the second-best view. Marsh view lots in most golf communities start in the high $100s and move up from there.

Chapter Ten

When a home feels like it has been customized to an owner's functional and aesthetic needs, the people who live there generally find it more appealing than the best five-star resort.

— Vern Yip

To Build Or Not To Build

Many clients prefer new homes, or at least a home of recent vintage. After all, who wants to deal with icky reconstruction of kitchens and bathrooms? Generally speaking, buyers are willing to spend a few thousand dollars more for a brand new home with granite counters, upgraded kitchen appliances, hardwood floors and other new accessories lacking in many 40-year-old houses.

Costs to Build Have Skyrocketed

But if you calculate the cost of a new home compared with one, say, built 25 years ago, you might find that the difference would be more than enough to pay for an entire houseful of upgrades in the resale home—with money left over for an initiation fee at the country club, airplane tickets for the kids and grandkids to visit, and perhaps an escape vacation during the heat of the summer or the darkest days of winter.

In recent years, a range of factors have conspired to push up the cost of new home construction relative to resale homes. The U.S. government's inability to come up with a revised and rational immigration policy has drained the construction industry of the only workers contractors could find to hammer nails on the roofs of new homes in the heat of the summer. That has created a labor shortage and pushed labor costs higher; it also has expanded the time it takes to get a house built.

One other major factor, according to experienced developer Ken Kirkman, is the explosion in the costs to prepare lots in new developments, or in new sections of existing developments.

"Those costs," Kirkman told me in early 2020, referring to his latest project, Carolina Colours in New Bern, NC, "add as much as $40,000 in hard and soft costs to the preparation of each lot, and that is without land cost. The $40,000 in costs is up from $15,000 per lot just 10 years ago."

The spread between the cost of a resale home and an identical new one has widened today, from the historical 5% to as much as 15% or more. "All in all, " said Kirkman, "new homes are about 25% more expensive than they were just five years ago."

Nevertheless, at the end of the summer in 2020, competition was intense for the relatively few golf homes on the market in high-quality communities.

"Prices in the lower half of [Landfall's] price points," Kirkman says of the Wilmington community he helped develop, "are getting quick, multiple offers and are selling, in some instances, above list." At the time he reported this to me, there were 40 properties for sale in Landfall. Typical, he said, is 100.

What You Should Expect to Pay for New

The price spread between a new home and old one, however, isn't always wide enough to dissuade purchase of a new one, especially if you can score a terrific home site at a bargain price. If you absolutely must have a home built to your own precise specifications, count on something like $200 per square foot in construction costs in many areas of the South. (Of course, if you insist on deluxe finishings, that cost will rise appropriately.) Assuming a lot that costs $100,000 and a standard three-bedroom, three-bath home of around 3,000 square feet, your brand new home will cost you approximately $700,000. A 2,000 square foot home would run to $500,000. (Note: Some golf communities dictate a minimum square footage for new homes, typically around 2,400 square feet.)

In my experience, the difference between buying someone else's home and building your own can be as much as 25% or more. The difference in cost can be narrower if the resale home needs updating or even more extensive renovations. Ultimately, any savings an existing home might provide may not be material to a couple that is set on their own personally designed layout and choice of fittings; but to others, the savings could make the difference in being able to afford to live in a particular community—or pay the initiation fee for the golf club.

Yet Land is Still Relatively Cheap

For those whose minds are set on building a home to their exact specifications, there is one factor still strongly in their favor. The prices of land have languished even during the run up in home prices. So even though costs to build have escalated, the overall costs of new home construction are not as dear as they might seem.

In many of the communities I have followed and can recommend, a choice selection of homesites in August 2020 were selling for under $10,000. Indeed, some lots in communities with mandatory club membership were selling as low as $1 in August 2020, especially in the high-end communities of Bluffton, SC. This is a repeat of what happened in 2008 when the local real estate market crashed. Some lots originally purchased for $400,000 during the early 2000s had appreciated 15% per year, and speculators—some of them already homeowners inside the gates—bought extra properties as investments. The $20,000 per year in club and HOA obligations per homesite posed no apparent risk at a time when the lots were appreciating as much as $60,000 annually.

But as we know about any investments, past performance is no indication of future results. As I write this, the Covid-19 pandemic has sent the economy into a tailspin and a number of homesites in mandatory membership communities are back in the bargain bin. (I counted more than a dozen $1 lots for sale in August 2020 in those luxurious Bluffton communities.)

Construction costs don't change by virtue of the cost of a homesite; therefore, the less expensive the land, the less the cost of the finished home. When the pandemic has fully passed, bargain properties will abound in some fine golf communities. The early bird will catch the worm in those lots. Just be mindful that the worm can turn at any time.

A Real Life Story of a Couple that Built

Bill and Karen Reutemann were Californians when they contacted me in 2009. Their timing was both propitious and intimidating, less than a year after the big recession began. Some golf communities had declared bankruptcies and others were in dubious shape. Bill and Karen were reasonably concerned with the financial viability of golf communities and the personal financial conditions of their developers. But they began their search at a time when prices in golf communities had softened, even plummeted in some places.

Their search took almost three years, but after a dozen visits or so to golf communities in the Southeast, they

TO BUILD OR NOT TO BUILD

believed that Governors Club in Chapel Hill, NC, near two major universities and sporting a Jack Nicklaus 27-hole layout, was the right place for them, and that a lot they saw and loved would provide a chance to build the home they had always dreamed of.

"Selecting an architect and general contractor, designing the house, getting the permits and everything else associated with a new home took one year and nine months," Bill told me. "We had never built a home before. It was a lot of work but we enjoyed the process.

"And we got everything we were looking for in a house."

Bill added that the only "regret" he and Karen had about the project was that "we could have been here sooner."

"Even though it may not seem like the right time to retire or sell your current home," he said, "it's never too soon to start looking." He says that although they had decided to relocate to a golf community, they spent two years looking at different locations. His excuse was that he was still working (in a second career).

"If I had it to do again," he adds, "I would have sped up the due diligence, bailed on the second career, and got here (Governors Club) ASAP."

Bill and Karen decided to rent a home at Governors Club to keep a close eye on construction of their home. I asked him if he thought that was entirely necessary.

"At the front end," he responded, "yes, because you are putting your team of architect and contractor and subcontractors together. And at the end, you want to make sure every detail has been attended to so, yes, you should be there then.

"But in the middle, during the height of construction, it wasn't really necessary."

The lesson here for those who might take on the building of their dream home, is to not be afraid of the process, consider being around at the front and back ends of the entire process, and understand that there is a way for you to have everything you want in your dream home.

GLORIOUS BACK NINE

Chapter Eleven

Remember, life is short, so do things that matter the most and have the courage to make the "tough decision" and to chase your dreams.
—Yama Mubtaker

The Home Stretch

At this point you have done all your research, considered which golf communities suit you best, refined the list of the top choices and identified the community for you. Now comes the easiest part—choosing a home.

Why "easiest?" For one thing, there is nothing subjective about how much you have to spend on a house. You know your budget. If you have, say, $600,000 to spend on a house, you will look only at homes listed up to around $630,000, mindful that a bit of negotiation is part of the song and dance with sellers. If you are looking to spend, say, $300,000, then a home at $315,000 could be your target. If you find a house whose owners have a sense of urgency, you might get up to 10% off the price. Those sellers who are not in a hurry may offer only a percent or two off their list price. On average, and assuming no extreme circumstances, expect up to 5% of wiggle room in the price, and never turn your back on a home you love for a percent or two more.

You Know What You Want. Grab It.

Another reason choosing a home will be relatively easy is that your own past experience will guide you. No couple lives in a house together for as long as decades without discussing, along the way, what they liked and didn't like about their home—or multiple homes. Those ongoing discussions through the years will inform your decision on requirements and nice-to-haves in your golf community home. Just remember that resale homes today are comparably less expensive than new homes. If you find a resale that comes close to what you want and certain features can be updated or renovated, seriously consider taking that approach. You are likely to save money and, in the end, have the house you want (and savings as well).

After you choose your golf community and return home, your real estate agent will be working hard to identify those houses for sale that match your criteria. Any real estate agency can set you up with a constant email alert showing relevant homes that come on the market in your price range. If one or more set off alarm bells for you, you can arrange a quick re-visit, tour the house and, if it's the one, make your offer.

An Organized Approach, a Quick Decision

But if on your first visit, you fall in love with a particular golf community, the process can be quick and extra-efficient. I worked with Jeff and Joni, a couple from Connecticut in 2019 who visited the community of Callawassie Island in Okatie, SC, after touring about a dozen others on the South Carolina and Georgia coasts (in two separate trips). They were super-organized and knew exactly what they were looking for in a golf community and a house. (When they first contacted me, they were concerned they each might not be on the same page in terms of criteria for a golf community; therefore, I asked them to fill out, and send to me, separately, checklists of their preferences. Fortunately, they matched up in all the most important areas.)

Callawassie Island, Okatie, SC   Photo by Larry Gavrich

On that first visit to Callawassie, they knew it was the golf community for them, and they looked at a number of houses there with the real estate agent I had recommended to work with them. During their visit, they identified three homes that suited them, and made an offer on one of them, then returned to Connecticut to wait. They didn't get their first choice, but their next offer, on house choice #2, was accepted. They sold their house in Connecticut a few days later, closed on the Callawassie house a month after that, and they were full-fledged members of the community a few days later.

That was quicker than most searches. But as we know in life, love at first sight rarely misleads.

GLORIOUS BACK NINE

Afterword

If you can dream it, you can do it.
—Walt Disney

You Did It

Your search for your dream golf home has been a lot like the game of golf itself. Having a strategy can overcome bad bounces and other unforeseen trip-ups on the golf course. And so it is in the search for a golf community home.

You now have the tools for an organized approach that will help you find your dream home on the course in a year or less. For those with either more time to search or who are not quite ready, everything on the preceding pages will work to your advantage when you start your search.

You just need to follow these steps to success:

- Ensure you and your significant other want the same things in a golf community home. You don't both have to be golf nuts. In fact, you don't have to play golf at all as long as you enjoy the social aspects of belonging to a club, manicured landscapes and the prospect that one of the biggest investments you will ever make is sound.

- Decide on geography before you start searching—coastal, mountains, lake or other.
- Pick a lifestyle: Lots of action and entertainment (near a city) or a noise- and pollution-free environment in a rural location; or somewhere in between.
- Determine your budget, for a house and its carrying costs, and stick to it. Include any private club initiation fees and dues in the budget calculations.
- Use the Internet to determine which golf communities have the amenities you want; do not search for specific homes in communities you haven't visited.
- Contact a professional real estate agent for those areas you target, preferably one who knows all the local golf communities. Your buyer's agent can answer questions about golf fees and homeowner costs before you commit to a visit.
- If a community or two stand out, consider taking advantage of their "Discovery Packages" which will provide lodging on site (in most cases) and access to golf and other member amenities. Play the course and use the clubhouse to get to know your potential neighbors.
- If you fall in love with a community, tour some homes in your price range with your real estate agent. If you don't find one you like, ask the agent to put you on an automated email list to send you new listings in your price range.
- When you find the home that matches your requirements, make a reasonable offer. Don't walk away from a home you love for a percentage point or two.
- And, finally, when you move to your new golf community, relax, enjoy the golf, the social activities and your new life. You've earned it.

YOU DID IT

GLORIOUS BACK NINE

Appendix A

Top Communties in the Southeast

Information below, including home and lot prices, was collected in August 2020. All listed golf communities have been visited by the author, except as noted with an *. In those cases, he relied on research and positive public reports to deem them worthy of including in this list. However, circumstances change, and it is always best when the exchange of money is involved to practice *caveat emptor*—buyer beware.

Virginia

Coastal

Bay Creek, Cape Charles
36 holes by Jack Nicklaus & Arnold Palmer
Condos from $284,000
Single-family homes from $399,000 (new)
Homesites from $70,000
Notes: Remote location on the Delmarva Peninsula, 30 minutes over the Chesapeake Bay Bridge & Tunnel from Norfolk, VA…a little over four hours drive from Washington and Philadelphia…Two miles of private beach on bay.

Colonial Heritage, Williamsburg
18 holes by Arthur Hills
Homes from $250,000
Notes: A 55+ age restricted community with lots of on-site activities. The golf course is excellent but tough, and some seniors may find the forced carries a bit much.

Ford's Colony, Williamsburg
54 holes by Dan Maples
Homes from $389,000
Notes: Homeowners association has managed the community since 2000. Golf club has been through multiple ownerships in last 10 years but appears to have stabilized now under ClubCorp.

Governor's Land at Two Rivers, Williamsburg
18 holes by Tom Fazio
Lots from $120,000
Homes from $465,000
Notes: Finishing holes on golf course run beside the historic James River. One of few members' only courses in the area.

Kingsmill, Williamsburg
36 holes by Pete Dye and Arnold Palmer
Lots from $235,000
Condos/townhomes from $145,000
Single-family homes from $325,000
Notes: A sprawling resort with a golf course good enough to have hosted both PGA and LPGA tour events.

Inland

Creighton Farms, Aldie
18 holes by Jack Nicklaus
Homes from $1 million+
Notes: Ultra-luxury less than an hour from nation's capital. Beautifully designed and conditioned course, with extra touches in practice area.

Dominion Valley, Haymarket
18 holes by Arnold Palmer
Condos from $339,000
Homes from $470,000
Notes: Community, which was built by Toll Brothers, is close to I-66, 75 minutes from Washington and just 20 minutes from Dulles International Airport. The club is managed by ClubCorp.

Fawn Lake, Fredericksburg
18 holes by Arnold Palmer
Lots from $65,000
Homes from $378,000
Notes: In historic Spotsylvania, 90 minutes from Washington, D.C. Don't expect to fawn over the lake until the 18th hole, where it appears for the first time.

Federal Club, Glen Allen
18 holes by Arnold Palmer
Lots from $180,000
Homes from $619,000
Notes: Original owners bankrupted during 2008 recession. Excellent private golf course continued to operate but began accepting daily fee play. Bentgrass greens and fairways.

Glenmore, Keswick
18 holes by John LaFoy.
Lots from $140,000
Homes from $499,000
Notes: Scottish influence notable throughout the community and on the golf course. Some residents are professors from nearby University of Virginia.

Kinloch, Manakin-Sabot
18 holes by Lester George
Lots from $405,000
Homes from $600,000
Notes: Architect George has designed some of the most dramatic layouts in the South, and Kinloch is right up there.

Old Trail, Crozet
18 holes by Jerry Kamis
Condos from $289,000
Homes from $475,000
Notes: Ark scene from the movie *Evan Almighty* was shot at Old Trail. Golf course is fun to play, with a few quirky design elements.

Spring Creek, Zion Crossroads
18 holes by Ed Carton
Lots from $50,000
Condos from $239,000
Homes from $319,000
Notes: Beautifully designed golf course threads through, but not too close, to homes of recent vintage. Community is between Richmond and Charlottesville, closer to the latter.

Mountain

The Virginian*, Bristol
18 holes by Tom Fazio
Lots from $65,000
Homes from $459,000
Notes: Long established higher-end community close to the Tennessee border.

Wintergreen Resort, Nellysford
45 holes by Ellis Maples and Rees Jones
Mountain Lots from $19,000
Valley Lots from $20,000
Mountain condos from $59,000
Mountain homes from $250,000
Valley homes from $315,000
Notes: Quintessential all-season resort, perfect year-round location for golfer/skiers. The Devil's Knob golf course at the top of the mountain is nominally private and focused on its members.

North Carolina

Coastal

Albemarle Plantation, Hertford
18 holes by Dan Maples
Lots from $5,000
Condos from $80,000
Homes from $245,000
Notes: Hertford, birthplace of pitching great Jim "Catfish" Hunter, is located on US Highway 17, the chief north/south route along the coast. Albemarle's golf club, Sound Links, bumps up against an expanse of water between the mainland and the Outer Banks.

Carolina Colours, New Bern
18 holes by Bill Love
Lots from $55,500
Homes from $338,000
Notes: Great golf course to "grow old" on, challenging yet fair. Friendly community where residents gather on most Friday nights for a meal and conversation. Original developer lives in the community.

Currituck Club, Corolla
18 holes by Rees Jones
Lots from $50,000
Condos from $275,000
Homes from $335,000
Notes: Golf course winds through maritime forests and above beach, with views of the ocean. On the north end of Outer Banks, close to four-wheel-drive beach with wild horses.

Governors Club, Chapel Hill
27 holes by Jack Nicklaus
Lots from $25,000
Homes from $360,000
Notes: Well-tended community with beautiful large rock outcroppings on rolling landscape. Involved members who keep the country club and community looking up to date.

Brunswick Forest, Leland
18 holes by Tim Cate
Lots from $78,500
Homes from $260,000
Notes: Just 10 minutes from downtown Wilmington. Deep-pocketed owner/developer. Mix of small homes on small lots, close to neighbors, plus estate homes. Golf course features lots of sand and is a treat to play.

Landfall, Wilmington
45 holes by Pete Dye & Jack Nicklaus
Lots from $219,000
Homes from $439,000
Notes: Ideally located between Wrightsville Beach on the Atlantic Ocean, and Wilmington—about 10 minutes from each. Golf courses are top quality; the Nicklaus 18 is the site of a major annual college tournament.

Porters Neck, Wilmington
18 holes by Tom Fazio
Lots from $95,000
Homes from $349,000
Notes: Formerly member-owned club was purchased by the McConnell Group in September 2020 and is now part of the McConnell portfolio of 13 courses in the Carolinas and Tennessee. Close to city of Wilmington and nearby beaches. Nicely landscaped with many mature trees and plantings.

River Landing, Wallace
36 holes by Clyde Johnston
Lots from $5,000
Homes from $175,000
Notes: Located just off I-40 which runs between Raleigh (75 minutes away) and Wilmington (45 minutes). Branch of Cape Fear River runs through community.

Ocean Ridge Plantation, Sunset Beach
72 holes by Tim Cate and Willard Byrd
Lots from $12,500
Homes from $380,000
Notes: Entrance just off US Highway 17 north of Myrtle Beach. Plenty of amenities including a beach club as well as four 18-hole golf courses.

Bald Head Island
18 holes by George Cobb
Lots from $40,000
Condos from $365,000
Homes from $499,000
Notes: Golf course designer Cobb produced the par 3 course at Augusta National. Bald Head offers many ¼ share (13-week) options for houses at prices that begin below $100,000. No autos on island; golf carts are ubiquitous mode of transportation. Continuous ferry to/from Southport on mainland 20 minutes away.

St. James Plantation, Southport
81 holes of golf by Nicklaus Design, P.B. Dye, Hale Irwin & Tim Cate
Lots from $25,000
Condos from $195,000
Homes from $280,000
Notes: Sprawling golf community with its own zip code. Loaded with amenities including beach club on nearby Oak Island, multiple pools, a large marina, three fitness centers and five restaurants.

Scotch Hall Preserve, Merry Hill
18 holes by Arnold Palmer
Lots from $64,000
Homes from $675,000
Notes: Located on the Albemarle Sound, Scotch Hall is located 19 miles from the historic and charming town of Edenton. The golf course features some beautiful views of the water.

Compass Pointe, Leland
18 holes by Rick Robbins
Lots from $83,500
Homes from $329,500
Notes: Compass Pointe had the misfortune of opening shortly before the 2008 recession and, of course, initial sales were slow in coming. But now, with a nice golf course in place and its location within a half hour of Wilmington and its beaches, Compass Pointe has hit its stride.

River's Edge Plantation, Shallotte
18 holes by Arnold Palmer
Lots from $11,000
Condos from $235,000
Homes from $400,000
Notes: The semi-private golf course hugs the Shallotte River and tidal marsh and features some dramatic holes. Private club on Holden Beach for residents.

Winding River Plantation*, Bolivia
27 holes by Fred Couples
Lots from $18,000
Condos from $175,000
Homes from $315,000
Notes: Mostly single-family homes (900) with just 60 condo units on 1,600 acres. Private club for residents on Holden Beach.

Inland

National Golf Club (Pinehurst #9), Pinehurst
18 holes by Jack Nicklaus
Lots from $100,000
Homes from $245,000
Notes: Club was purchased by the Pinehurst Resort and is now the resort's 9th golf course. Full members at Pinehurst have access to all nine golf courses, including the famed #2. Membership is conditional on being a resident of one of Pinehurst's communities.

Cypress Landing, Chocowinity
18 holes by Bill Love & Ault, Clark & Associates
Lots from $9,900
Homes from $259,000
Notes: Fine, yet under-the-radar golf community on an extension of the Pamlico River, close to Greenville, East Carolina University and a huge medical center. Reasonable real estate prices and golf fees.

Uwharrie Point, New London
18 holes by Tom Fazio (Old North State Club)
Lots from $500
Homes from $328,000
Notes: If you love peace and quiet, and outstanding golf, you will find it at Uwharrie Point. Halfway between Charlotte and Greensboro, about an hour from each. Golf club is owned and managed by McConnell Group; members have access to the group's excellent dozen golf courses across the Carolinas.

Ironwood, Greenville
18 holes by Lee Trevino
Lots from $49,000
Homes from $428,000
Notes: Traditional-style neighborhood with a golf course, one of the few credited to former great tour player, Trevino. Close to university and large medical center.

Brook Valley, Greenville
18 holes by Ellis Maples
Homes from $236,500
Notes: Another McConnell Golf Group club that confers member access to a dozen other terrific courses. Brook Valley is located within a few miles of East Carolina University and a large medical center.

Salem Glen, Clemmons
18 holes by Jack Nicklaus Design
Lots from $70,000
Homes from $394,000
Notes: At a weekday senior rate of $32 to play, it won't be worth it to join the semi-private club unless you plan to play three or more times a week. The publicly accessible Tanglewood Championship course, site of the 1974 PGA championship, is just a few miles away.

Chapel Ridge, Pittsboro
18 holes by Fred Couples and Bob Moore
Lots from $40,000
Homes from $425,000
Notes: Reasonably priced memberships confer access to two other fine golf courses in the area. Real estate prices comparably reasonable for the Chapel Hill area.

The Preserve at Jordan Lake, Chapel Hill
18 holes by Davis Love III
Lots from $55,000
Homes from $550,000
Notes: A companion community to Chapel Ridge with a golf course that is a magnitude tougher. Membership here confers access to Chapel Ridge and one other local course.

Mountains

Bear Lake Reserve, Tuckasegee
9 holes by Nicklaus Design
Lots from $47,000
Villas from $425,000
Homes from $375,000
Notes: Breathtaking par 29 golf course at summit of the mountain, with green fees complimentary for residents. Beautiful active lake compliments golf; summer mountain breezes a nice compliment to winters in Florida.

Balsam Mountain Preserve, Sylva
18 holes by Arnold Palmer
Lots from $129,000
Cabins from $600,000
Homes from $700,000
Notes: The best land in the community was given over to the golf course at Balsam Mountain's summit. Tilted and edge-of-the-mountain fairways make the course feel as intimidating as it is breathtaking.

Connestee Falls, Brevard
18 holes by George Cobb
Lots from $5,000
Homes from $219,000
Notes: Long-established community in the mountains near the popular town of Brevard. The golf course is cut through the wooded mountainside, with lots of changes in elevation.

Mountaintop*, Cashiers
18 holes by Tom Fazio
Lots from $249,000
Homes from $1.4 million
Notes: Ultra-deluxe mountain community with top-rated golf course and lake activities in very private setting.

GLORIOUS BACK NINE

Cliffs at Walnut Cove, Arden
18 holes by Jack Nicklaus
Lots from $149,000
Homes from $985,000
Notes: The only Cliffs community outside South Carolina is one of its most luxurious, and well located about 20 minutes from the vibrant city of Asheville.

Champion Hills, Hendersonville
18 holes by Tom Fazio
Lots from $19,000
Villas from $319,000
Homes from $469,000
Notes: Designer Fazio moved with his wife to Hendersonville in the early 1980s and set up his architecture business there. He and Mrs. Fazio are members of the club. Club and community are well run by engaged and organized residents.

Kenmure, Flat Rock
18 holes by Joe Lee
Lots from $15,000
Condos from $292,000
Homes from $425,000
Notes: Not as well-known as some of its neighboring golf communities but well established and reasonably priced. Course designer Lee translated quite well his experience with flat Florida courses to one of his rare mountain layouts.

Rumbling Bald, Lake Lure
36 holes by Dan Maples and W.B. Lewis
Lots from $100 (not a typo)
Condos from $48,000
Homes from $199,000
Notes: Large (3,000+ acres) and active resort with many rental opportunities to generate income. You will share the community with many transient vacationers, but the prices certainly are right.

Reems Creek, Weaverville
18 holes by Hawtree & Sons
Lots from $54,500
Homes from $550,000
Notes: Course designers do most of their work in the United Kingdom, and the Reems Creek layout shows many of the touches of both Scottish links and parkland courses.

Mountain Air, Burnsville
18 holes by Scott Poole
Lots from $30,500
Condos $159,500
Homes from $399,000
Notes: The golf course shares its top of mountain location with an air strip. Pilots and golfers both have exhilarating views, as do those having a beverage or food in the perfectly situated clubhouse

South Carolina

Coastal

Grande Dunes, Myrtle Beach
36 holes by Roger Rulewich and Nick Price
Lots from $114,000
Condos from $144,000
Homes from $331,000
Notes: One public, one private golf course (managed by the McConnell Group), both along the Intracoastal Waterway. Many Grand Dunes single-family homes have a classic Florida feel, with terracotta roofing and dramatic entryways.

Barefoot Resort, North Myrtle Beach
72 holes by Love III, Greg Norman, TomFazio & Pete Dye
Lots from $155,000
Condos from $131,000
Homes from $258,000
Notes: Plenty of excellent golf, but you will share it with vacationing families and buddy golfers down for a week or long weekend. Still, Barefoot is in the middle of all the action in North Myrtle Beach.

Wachesaw Plantation, Murrells Inlet
18 holes by Tom Fazio
Lots from $90,000
Homes from $410,000
Notes: This is an early, classic Fazio course. Wachesaw is located on the "wrong" side (west) of US Highway 17 but only two miles from beaches and Restaurant Row, a large collection of mostly seafood restaurants. Local hospital is within two minutes as well.

The Reserve at Litchfield, Litchfield Beach
18 holes by Greg Norman
Lots from $140,000
Homes from $635,000
Notes: Includes marina on the Waccamaw River. Reserve is 5 minutes to the private-access beach on the Atlantic. Club is owned and managed by the McConnell Group, giving members access to a dozen other excellent private courses in the Carolinas and Tennessee.

Pawleys Plantation, Pawleys Island
18 holes by Jack Nicklaus
Lots from $85,500
Condos from $170,000
Homes from $260,000
Notes: Your author and his wife have owned a vacation condo here since 2000. The golf course "explodes" out onto the marsh on the back nine. It is just six minutes from the front gate to one of the nicest public beaches on the

east coast. For at-home chefs, there are five supermarkets within five miles.

DeBordieu Colony, Georgetown
18 holes by Pete Dye
Lots from $69,000
Condos from $525,000
Homes from $775,000
Notes: An under-appreciated golf community in that its residents can enjoy both golf and their own private beach. Community is surrounded north and south by conservation land.

Charleston National, Mt. Pleasant
18 holes by Rees Jones
Lots from $160,000
Condos from $290,000
Homes from $385,000
Notes: Mt. Pleasant is one of the fastest growing suburbs (Charleston) on the east coast, and plenty of retail and other services have followed suit. To be within a short drive of one of the best restaurant cities in the South is a treat.

Dunes West, Mt. Pleasant
18 holes by Arthur Hills
Lots from $179,000
Homes from $350,000
Notes: Sprawling community with fine golf course at its core feels more like a neighborhood than a planned community. Twenty minutes to Charleston and the beaches on Isle of Palms.

Rivertowne, Mt. Pleasant
18 holes by Arnold Palmer
Lots from $170,000
Homes from $465,000
Notes: Just over the Ravenel Bridge from Charleston, the community is adjacent to the Wando River. Dual membership with Snee Farm, a few miles away. (See below)

Snee Farm, Mt. Pleasant
18 holes by George Cobb
Condos from $190,000
Homes from $349,500
Notes: Mature neighborhood with homes quite fairly priced, some in need of updating. Central to everything in Mt. Pleasant.

Wild Dunes, Isle of Palms
36 holes by Tom Fazio
Lots from $597,000
Condos from $120,000
Homes from $549,500
Notes: Two distinctly different layouts, one oceanside and the other by the harbor; ocean links finishes on the beach. Popular resort in all seasons and just 20 minutes to Charleston.

Daniel Island, North Charleston
36 holes by Tom Fazio and Rees Jones
Lots from $375,000
Condos from $249,500
Homes from $615,000
Notes: The best of both worlds; an island separated slightly from the mainland and just off the Interstate and, yet, 15 minutes to downtown Charleston. Not cheap but a complete, smartly organized community with most necessary services on site, and two highly rated golf courses.

Kiawah Island Club, Kiawah Island
36 holes (private) by Tom Watson and Tom Fazio
90 holes (public) by Clyde Johnston, Jack Nicklaus, Gary Player, Tom Fazio and Pete Dye (the famed Ocean Course).
Lots from $98,500
Condos from $355,000
Homes from $649,000
Notes: Beautiful beaches, splendid golf, the ultimate combination of the two. Kiawah is a popular resort at peak seasons, and only two of the golf courses are strictly for members only (with initiation fee over $100,000).

Brier's Creek, Johns Island
18 holes by Rees Jones
Lots from $149,500
Homes (no homes for sale August 2020)
Notes: Brier's Creek got off to a slow start in terms of sales in the early 2000s, but the quality of the Rees Jones course at its core was never in doubt. Small community with homes (when available) priced at $1 million plus.

Seabrook Island, Seabrook Island
36 holes by Robert Trent Jones Sr and Willard Byrd
Lots from $39,000
Condos from $110,000
Homes from $395,000
Notes: Located just south of Kiawah Island, not as deluxe but prices are more reasonable. Golf is excellent on site and five of the courses on Kiawah are open to public play. About 45 minutes from Charleston.

Callawassie Island, Okatie
27 holes by Tom Fazio
Lots from $2,500
Homes from $170,000
Notes: Ideally located between Bluffton/Hilton Head Island and the charming Southern town of Beaufort, yet secluded behind the front gate. Prices are especially reasonable for such a high-quality community. Club members are obligated to pay dues until they find someone to purchase their membership (and their property).

Spring Island, Okatie
18 holes by Arnold Palmer/Ed Seay
Lots from $35,000
Cottages from $475,000
Homes from $1.1 million
Notes: One of the most beautiful golf courses in South Carolina, lavished with loving care by its well-to-do members. The community is secluded in a beautiful, marsh-oriented setting, dripping with live oak trees.

Dataw Island, St. Helena
36 holes by Tom Fazio and Arthur Hills
Lots from $1 (not a typo)
Villas from $160,000
Homes from $230,000
Notes: Well-established community with two fine golf courses and some of the most reasonably priced real estate anywhere (many homes in need of a little bit of freshening after a few decades). "Remote," but only 20 minutes to charming Beaufort and the same to an Atlantic beach.

Edisto Island*, Edisto Island
18 holes by Tom Jackson
Lots from $46,000
Condos from $123,000
Homes from $385,000
Notes: Edisto is not easy to get to—a good 40 minutes from US Highway 17—which is part of its charm. Still some beach acreage available for those with a dream of a home on the ocean.

Fripp Island*, Fripp Island
36 holes by George Cobb and Davis Love III
Lots from $69,000
Condos from $143,000
Homes from $329,000
Notes: Remote, yet just 30 minutes from Beaufort and with golf and beach all in one.

Colleton River, Bluffton
36 holes by Jack Nicklaus and Pete Dye
Lots from $1 (not a typo)
Homes from $487,500
Notes: Membership is obligatory for all residents. Nicklaus course greens were the fastest your author has played in 10 years (and that's a compliment). Just a few minutes over the bridge to the Hilton Head Island beaches.

Berkeley Hall, Bluffton
36 holes by Tom Fazio
Lots from $1 (not a typo)
Homes from $329,000
Notes: One of the big three in Bluffton (the others are Colleton River and Belfair). Obligatory membership for all residents keeps golf course well-funded through good times and bad.

Belfair, Bluffton
36 holes by Tom Fazio
Lots from $5,000
Homes from $439,000
Notes: Like its companions Berkeley Hall and Colleton River, membership for residents is compulsory. Bluffton is a bustling town with plenty of services, including a large Tanger Outlets retail complex.

Moss Creek, Bluffton
36 holes by Tom Fazio
Lots from $100,000
Condos from $220,000
Homes from $335,000
Notes: The granddaddy of the big, multi-golf course communities in Bluffton. Located almost at the foot of the bridge to Hilton Head Island, making it a short drive to the island's beaches and other attractions.

Wexford, Hilton Head Island
18 holes by Willard Byrd/Renovated by Arnold Palmer
Condos from $499,000
Homes from $499,000
Notes: Golf course, dramatically and artfully renovated in 2011 by Brandon Johnson, from the Arnold Palmer design shop.

Indigo Run, Hilton Head Island
18 holes by Jack Nicklaus and Jack Nicklaus II
Lots from $110,000
Homes from $643,500
Notes: Members of Indigo Run, which is managed by ClubCorp, also have access to the Golden Bear Golf Club (public) across the street, also managed by ClubCorp.

Inland

Cliffs at Keowee Vineyards, Sunset
18 holes by Tom Fazio
Lots from $10,000
Homes from $550,000
Notes: One of three Cliffs communities on Lake Keowee, Vineyards is arguably the best golf course of all the Cliffs' seven layouts. Its par 3 17th hole, from an elevated tee box to a green backed by a big beautiful part of the lake, is the most dramatic one-shotter anywhere.

The Reserve at Lake Keowee, Sunset
18 holes by Jack Nicklaus
Lots from $1 (not a typo)
Homes from $560,000
Notes: Well-organized community developed by group of local professional men. Conservative management helped keep the community thriving through the 2008 recession and poised it for impressive growth. Golf course has hosted [Web.com](Web.com) tour event.

Keowee Key, Salem
18 holes by George Cobb/renovated by Richard Mandell
Lots from $4,000
Condos from $105,000
Homes from $213,000
Notes: Some of the most reasonably priced real estate on any lake in the east. Remotely located about 20 minutes from the university town of Clemson.

Woodcreek Farms, Elgin
18 holes by Tom Fazio
Lots from $115,500
Homes from $285,000
Notes: Located just 20 minutes from Columbia and the huge University of South Carolina campus. Membership at Woodcreek confers full access to Wildewood's golf course just four miles away (see below).

Wildewood, Columbia
18 holes by Russell Breeden
Lots from $30,000
Homes from $234,000
Notes: Twenty minutes from University of South Carolina as well as all services in Columbia, the state capital. Reciprocal membership with Woodcreek Farms golf community.

Cobblestone Park, Blythewood
27 holes by P.B. Dye; renovated by Lee Janzen
Lots from $8,400
Homes from $260,000
Notes: Solidly designed public golf course. Community got off to a rocky start in the early 2000s when developer Bobby Ginn oversold its promise (and the value of its properties). Repurposed after Ginn bankruptcy by national builder D.R. Horton with efficiently built and lower priced homes. Community has regained its footing.

Chanticleer (Greenville Country Club), Greenville
18 holes by Robert Trent Jones, Sr.
Homes from $825,000
Notes: Perennial top-five golf course in all of golf rich South Carolina. The community is inside the city boundaries and one of its most upscale. Members of Chanticleer enjoy privileges at club's Riverside Course four miles away (see below).

Riverside (Greenville Country Club), Greenville
18 holes originally by William Langford, later worked on by George Cobb and John LaFoy, and redesigned by Brian Silva in 2007.
Homes from $710,000
Notes: Renovation by Silva followed a classic motif, including a "punchbowl green." Surrounding community is more like a neighborhood with a golf course than a planned development. Members can play both their course and the Chanticleer course four miles away.

Cherokee Valley, Travelers Rest
18 holes by P.B. Dye
Lots from $35,000
Homes from $460,000
Notes: Nicely landscaped community in which developers showed great respect for the indigenous trees. However, the golf course was designed with many funneled fairways in such a way as to minimize the views of the Blue Ridge Mountains beyond—unconsciously, we presume.

Pebble Creek, Taylors
36 holes by Tom Jackson
Condos from $160,000
Homes from $270,000
Notes: Pebble Creek is a unique blend of one public and one private course that share the same clubhouse and pro shop. Private club membership, which is quite reasonably priced, provides no-green-fee golf at both. Active men's group is great way to get to know your neighbors.

Thornblade Club, Greer
18 holes by Tom Fazio
Lots from $165,500 (very few)
Townhouses from $460,000
Homes from $725,000
Notes: A family-oriented club that is also retiree-friendly. Less a planned community than a neighborhood. PGA player Lucas Glover, whose grandparents lived beside the course, honed his game at Thornblade; Jay Haas, former PGA luminary and father of Bill Haas, PGA Tour player, was founding member of Thornblade and still lives there.

Green Valley, Greenville
18 holes by George Cobb
Homes from $569,500
Notes: Golf club has been owned and managed by one family that has invested more than $4 million in improvements over the last decade, with no member assessments. It is an extremely member-friendly club adjacent to a mature neighborhood.

Cliffs Valley, Travelers Rest
18 holes by Ben Wright
Lots from $30,000
Homes from $475,000
Notes: One of the more established Cliffs communities not far from Greenville. "Valley" is an apt name for the golf course as it is surrounded by higher elevations, with many homes dotting the mountainsides. Must declare membership (social or full golf) at time of purchase.

Cliffs at Mountain Park, Travelers Rest
18 holes by Gary Player
Lots from $100,000
Condos from $289,000
Homes from $595,000
Notes: Splendid Player layout that runs along the North Saluda River on a mostly flat piece of land surrounded by mountains. One of the more recently developed of the Cliffs communities, and an easy drive to Greenville. Membership provides access to all seven Cliffs courses in SC and NC.

Grand Harbor, Ninety-Six
18 holes by Davis Love III
Lots from $12,500
Homes from $425,000
Notes: Located on the beautiful, manmade Lake Greenwood a few miles from the college town of Greenwood. The Davis Love design is unusual in that he used replicas of brick ruins of a nearby Revolutionary War fort as "sculptures" on the course.

Woodside, Aiken
36 holes by Nicklaus Design and Fuzzy Zoeller
Lots from $17,000
Homes from $235,000
Notes: Sprawling, popular community near the charming town of Aiken, famed for its equestrian orientation. Country club is managed by Troon Golf and confers access for members to play at any of Troon's other 250 courses. Those who can't get enough golf can also join the Woodside Plantation club nearby with another 45 holes of golf managed by ClubCorp.

Mount Vintage, North Augusta
18 holes by Tom Jackson
Lots from $15,000
Homes from $340,000
Notes: Mount Vintage went through some tough times during the 2008 recession as the golf course was taken over by a bank and conditions went from great, when it opened in 2000, to lousy in 2015. But there has been a turnaround in years since, lawsuits have been settled and the golf course, which has echoes of Augusta National, is doing fine once again.

Cedar Creek, Aiken
18 holes by Arthur Hills
Lots from $8,000
Homes from $279,000
Notes: Some of the most reasonably priced real estate in the area, given the fine Hills layout, mature landscaping throughout the community and engaged residents, many of whom are scientists who work at the nearby Savannah River Project.

Savannah Lakes Village, McCormick
36 holes by Tom Clark
Lots from $1,000
Condos from $135,000
Homes from $163,000
Notes: You are not likely to find a golf community by a lake with more than one golf course and real estate prices as low as at Savannah Lakes. Yes, it is located some distance from sizable towns, and you will have to plan your shopping excursions. But you won't be lonely, as the community has attracted 2,000 others and has plenty to keep its residents on site (including a bowling alley).

Mountains

Cliffs at Glassy, Landrum
18 holes by Tom Jackson
Lots from $2,400
Homes from $334,000
Notes: One of the original Cliffs communities and the golf course, especially the views from the mountain top, certainly was a selling point. The farthest north of the Cliffs group, almost in North Carolina, but its remote, mountain location is part of its charm.

Links O' Tryon*, Campobello
18 holes by Tom Jackson
Lots from $30,000
Homes from $395,000
Notes: Both a resort and golf community.

Georgia

Coastal

The Landings, Savannah
108 holes by Willard Byrd, Arnold Palmer, Tom Fazio and Arthur Hills
Lots from $65,000
Condos from $279,000
Homes from $319,000
Notes: Possibly the most complete golf community, with just about everything to recommend it, starting with six excellent golf courses; a 45-year track history of excellent management and residential harmony; more than 100 clubs and activities; and a location just 20 minutes from an interesting, full-service city. If it lacks one thing, it is proximity to a beach, which is 45 minutes away (or a 10-minute boat ride).

Savannah Quarters, Pooler
18 holes by Greg Norman
Lots from $102,000
Condos from $194,000
Homes from $248,000
Notes: Located just 10 miles from Savannah and close to the junction of two interstates, Savannah Quarters is divided into discrete neighborhoods of single-family homes and townhomes. Norman was called in to totally redesign Bob Cupp's original layout, and his Medallist Company to further develop the community. But as the recession of 2008 neared, Medallist's plans stalled and a few years later, the company sold its interest. The next developers have grown the community significantly since then.

Ford Plantation, Richmond Hill
18 holes by Pete Dye
Lots from $15,000
Homes from $299,000
Notes: Most homes are priced well above $500,000 and nearly half above $1 million. This is ultra-deluxe living beside the Oconee River, with an outstanding Dye layout and a load of antebellum atmosphere. The Ford in the name is Henry Ford; he and his wife Clara spent a lot of time at their Southern vacation home.

Osprey Cove, St. Marys
18 holes by Mark McCumber
Lots from $17,500
Homes from $225,000
Notes: St. Marys is a charming small port city with a ferry to Cumberland Island, where wild horses roam and John Kennedy Jr. was married. Osprey Cove is located about 45 minutes from Jacksonville, should a night out in a big city be in order.

Frederica*, St. Simons
18 holes by Tom Fazio
Lots from $235,000
Homes from $1.8 million
Notes: The private golf course is festooned with more than 1,000 live oak trees, providing the ultimate in Low Country style. The style of Southern hospitality is carried throughout the amenities offered at this unique community.

Inland

Reynolds Lake Oconee, Greensboro
108 holes of golf by Jack Nicklaus, Tom Fazio, Bob Cupp, Jim Engh and Rees Jones
Lots from $15,000
Condos from $310,000
Homes from $510,000
Notes: Reynolds offers a smorgasbord of memberships where you can pair two courses, five courses or all six together. This might be the most financially stable community anywhere, given that it is owned and managed by Metropolitan Life Insurance Company.

Cuscowilla, Eatonton
18 holes by Bill Coore and Ben Crenshaw
Lots from $99,000
Homes from $279,000
Notes: The golf course was built in the modern era but has a classic feel all the way around. Some rentals on the property mean you will share the golf course with vacationers, but it is worth it to play there more often than others.

Harbor Club, Greensboro
18 holes by Tom Weiskopf & Jay Morrish
Lots from $24,500
Homes from $275,000
Notes: A little ways down Lake Oconee from the much larger Reynolds community, Harbor Club is family owned and family oriented. The golf course is very good and open to outside play. Baseball Hall of Famer Mickey Mantle once lived there.

Riverwood Plantation*, Evans
27 holes by Jack Nicklaus, Gary Player & Arnold Palmer
Homes from $185,000
Notes: The Champions Retreat golf course is unique in that nine holes were designed by each of the golfing greats. The courses span the bluffs, marshland and the middle of the Savannah River.

Mountains

Currahee Club, Toccoa
18 holes by Jim Fazio
Lots from $45,000
Homes from $385,000
Notes: One of the more recent golf communities in the Southeast, which means it opened just before the 2008 recession. That was a bit of a setback, but given the beautiful views of the mountains and Lake Hartwell from many of the properties and the dramatically laid out golf course, Currahee is attracting a lot of interest.

Old Toccoa Farm*, Toccoa
18 holes by Bunker Hill Golf
Lot prices not available
Home prices not available
Notes: At just over 400 acres, Old Toccoa is not a large community but it does span more than ¾ of a mile of the Toccoa River.

Big Canoe*, Jasper
27 holes by Joe Lee
Lots from $5,000
Condos from $135,000
Homes from $179,000
Notes: Located about 75 minutes from Atlanta. Designer Lee is known mostly for Florida courses, but he has shown his creativity on a few choice mountain and foothills layouts.

Florida

Coastal (east)

Amelia Island Plantation, Amelia Island
36 holes by Pete Dye (resort) and Tom Fazio (members)
Lots from $75,000
Condos from $335,000
Homes from $540,000
Notes: This is a resort, make no mistake about it, very popular during all seasons but, of course, mostly in winter. Long Cove is the private club located away from the resort activities.

Queen's Harbour, Jacksonville
18 holes by Mark McCumber
Lots from $150,000
Condos from $495,000
Homes from $438,000
Notes: Strong golf and boating atmosphere as the Intracoastal Waterway runs through the community. Golf club is managed by ClubCorp, which provides access for members to more than 200 other courses.

Hammock Beach*, Palm Coast
36 holes by Jack Nicklaus & Tom Watson
Lots from $90,000
Condos from $215,000
Homes from $539,000
Notes: Between the Atlantic Ocean and Intracoastal Waterway, so count on many water views from both golf course and homes. Community is nicely sized at 1,000 acres with adjacent nature preserves and two miles of beach.

Sawgrass Country Club*, Ponte Vedra Beach
27 holes by Ed Seay
Condos from $220,000
Homes from $869,000
Notes: Not to be confused with TPC Sawgrass, home of the Player's Championship and a golf community in its own right. Sawgrass CC is private whereas TPC gets a lot of transient traffic because of its famous golf course.

Pointe West, Vero Beach
18 holes by John Sanford
Condos from $194,500
Homes from $210,000
Notes: Under new ownership since 2019, the community is in a quiet area of Vero but not so far away that shopping and other services are a bother.

Grand Harbor, Vero Beach
36 holes by Pete Dye & Joe Lee
Condos from $176,500
Homes from $460,000
Notes: As the name implies, Grand Harbor has a strong orientation to seafaring, featuring a 144 boat slip and two-inlet access to the ocean. The two golf courses reflect the diversity of styles of their architects.

Willoughby, Stuart
18 holes by Arthur Hills
Homes from $255,000
Notes: Willoughby advertises proudly that it is condo-free, just single-family homes. Depending on neighborhood, two HOA fees might be required.

Coastal (west)

Lakewood Ranch, Lakewood Ranch
54 holes by Arnold Palmer (36) & Rick Robbins
Lots from $100,000
Condos from $168,000
Homes from $250,000
Notes: A master planned community close to Bradenton built on a former timber ranch. At 8,500 acres it is huge but separated into seven "villages" and multiple neighborhoods, each with its own character.

The Concession*, Bradenton
18 holes by Jack Nicklaus/Tony Jacklin
Lots from $255,000
Homes from $1.1 million
Notes: Named for the famous moment at the Ryder Cup when Nicklaus conceded a tying putt to Jacklin. Community features just 236 homesites, many still available, on its 1,200 acres.

Palm Aire, Sarasota
36 holes by Dick Wilson & Joe Lee
Condos from $159,000
Homes from $299,000
Notes: Some of the earliest televised golf was beamed from Palm Aire. Wide range of housing options, close to shopping, entertainment and other services.

TOP COMMUNTIES IN THE SOUTHEAST

River Strand*, Bradenton
27 holes by Arthur Hills
Condos from $170,000
Homes from $425,000
Notes: Developed by nationally known Lennar corporation, River Strand is one of their "bundled" communities, meaning that your HOA dues also pay for your membership in the country club.

Laurel Oak, Sarasota
36 holes by Gary Player & Rees Jones
Homes from $475,000
Notes: Close to Siesta Key's famous beaches and shopping. Nice combination of empty nesters and families. Most homes sited on good-sized lots give the community a spacious feel.

Longboat Key, Longboat Key
45 holes by Willard Byrd & Ron Garl
Lots from $208,000
Condos from $285,000
Homes from $500,000
Notes: Beautiful location surrounded by water yet not too far from the bustling town of Sarasota. Busy little island during the winter.

Prestancia, Sarasota
36 holes by Robert van Hagge & Ron Garl/Mike Souchak
Condos from $165,000
Homes from $395,000
Notes: Now a Tournament Players complex, in its early days the community played host to the Seniors' Tour of the PGA. TPC members receive privileges at other TPC courses around the country.

Venice Country Club*, Venice
18 holes by Ted McAnlis
Lots from $74,000
Condos from $203,000
Homes from $275,000
Notes: Club membership is attached to each property; every resident has a say in the operation of the club and golf course. This is the only golf community in Venice that is member owned and managed.

Pelican Pointe*, Venice
27 holes by Ted McAnlis
Condos from $225,000
Homes from $309,000
Notes: The community comprises 1,355 homesites and villas, with an abundant number of lakes and many water views from homes. The original 18 holes opened in 1995; the most recent nine debuted in 2002.

Heritage Bay, Naples
27 holes by Gordon Lewis/Jed Azinger
Condos from $170,000
Homes from $500,000
Notes: A Lennar golf community which means golf is bundled into your HOA payments. Practice area features unique "aqua" driving range with floating golf balls and a target in the middle of the lake.

Mediterra, Naples
36 holes by Tom Fazio
Coach homes from $639,000
Homes from $875,500
Notes: Mediterra is the high end in Naples. Member owned, more than 1,000 of its 1,700 acres have been set aside for lush landscaping and preserved spaces.

Audubon, Naples
18 holes by Joe Lee
Homes from $575,000
Notes: "The only gated Gulf side country club in Naples," according to the community literature. The 35,000 square foot clubhouse is huge but, in bright pink, was a bit overwhelming when I visited. The club recently opened a new 19,000 square foot "lifestyle" center at a cost of $7 million; it includes tennis, fitness equipment and a casual outdoor dining area.

Imperial Club Estates, Naples
18 holes by Arthur Hills & Ward Northrup
Condos from $280,000
Homes from $380,000
Notes: A mature community with a grown-in feel to it. Pretty much a golf-only country club with a fine clubhouse and among the most reasonable fee structures in Naples.

Esplanade*, Naples
18 holes by Chris Wilczynski
Condos from $273,000
Homes from $899,000
Notes: A rare golf community opened after the recession of 2008. Well-regarded national developer Taylor Morrison is involved.

Vineyards, Naples
36 holes by Mark McCumber & Bill Amick
Condos from $189,000
Homes from $325,000
Notes: The 38 neighborhoods of Vineyards comprise just about every type of home option, from condos and coach homes to single-family estate homes that sell for $1 million plus. A huge clubhouse dwarfs the adjacent pools and tennis court. A 70-bed medical facility is adjacent to the community.

GLORIOUS BACK NINE

Appendix B

Supportive Information

Since Baby Boomers make up a huge percentage of the population, many articles in the mainstream media address the issue of retirement. The sources below may not be as well known as those major media but offer concentrated advice and data for those contemplating retirement, as well as those of us already there.

Comparisons State to State

Kiplinger.com—Excellent, easy to follow advice and comparisons of states by their overall taxation rates, not just income tax.

United Van Lines Survey Results (https://www.united-vanlines.com/newsroom/movers-study-2019)—A truly objective assessment of where people are moving in the U.S. from a company that moves them.

BestPlaces.net—Using census and other data, compares cities by their cost of living rates and other factors. However, the richest benefit from the data now requires a modest subscription.

Pre-Retirement and Retiree Financial Issues

NerdWallet.com—Loads of straightforward advice for retirees and those planning to join the ranks.

Investopedia—I have linked to a specific article at the site because of its importance for many of you who will be reading this book: "Top Retirement Savings Tips for 54 to 65 Year Olds." If you are impressed with the advice, there is more at the site. https://www.investopedia.com/retirement/top-retirement-savings-tips-55-to-64-year-olds/

Fidelity—Full disclosure: Your author has been a Fidelity customer since early in his corporate career. I have always been impressed with their customer service and advice. Their retirement section is loaded with just such advice. http://Fidelity.com

Marketwatch—Plenty of retirement oriented articles that include practical advice. http://Marketwatch.com

The Balance—Wide range of information and advice, with a retirement planning section that is easy to follow and helpful. http://TheBalance.com

Mapping Out an Itinerary

Google.com/maps—There are many online mapping programs, but I have found that Google's offering is as easy to use as any. Simply open the program and add an initial destination. You might start, for example, with the airport you will fly to and from your home before driving to the area's golf communities. Or, if you are driving from home, just plug your home address into the Google Maps search box, then click "Directions" and enter your first stop at your destination (likely a hotel or the first golf community you intend to visit). From there, just click on the "Add destination" button and Google will map out your itinerary. Finish by adding your home for the return trip.

Appendix C

Helpful Reminders

Buyer Agents' Responsibilities

- Help you find the property that matches your requirements
- Assist you in the buying process, including preparation and review of all documents and paperwork
- Walk you through each property you identify
- Submit and negotiate offers on your behalf
- Refer you to reliable local professionals (e.g. mortgage and insurance companies, title companies, architects, contractors)
- Ensure required and proper insurances are in place
- Act as an impartial advisor to ensure your interests are served*

* Dual agency is legal in some states, where one agency or agent might represent both the buyer and seller of a property. Although any agent has a fiduciary responsibility to support your best interests, try to avoid any potential

conflict and engage a buyer's agent who does not also list homes in the area you are targeting.

Key Golf Community Documents to Review

- Documents of Incorporation of the Development
- Bylaws of the HOA and Golf Club (if relevant)
- Annual and Quarterly Financial Reports
- Covenants, conditions and restrictions (CC&R)
- HOA Communications to members (including newsletters)
- Golf Course Covenants
- Golf Course Deed
- Transfer of Rights to the Golf Course from the developer to the HOA (if relevant)

Appendix D

Your Home Search Checklist

Try to work through the items below pretty much in order as one decision can lead to the next. As you do, consider which items are "must haves," which are "nice to haves" and which are not important.

Choose One Geographic Location

- Coastal
- Mountains
- Lake or River
- Inland

Choose One General Location

- Near Urban (i.e. plenty of services such as hospitals, entertainment venues, restaurants, major airports)
- Ex-Urban (within 45 minutes of a city)
- Rural (quiet, little traffic or pollution, 45 minutes plus from city)

What Kind of View Would You Like from Your House?

(Rank order)
- Water
- Golf Course
- Wooded

Preferred # of Golf Courses on Site

- One
- Two
- Three or more
- Golf on property not important

Real Estate Budget

(incl. club initiation fee and homesite + construction costs, if planning to build)

Choose One

- $200,000 to $400,000
- $400,000 to $600,000
- $600,000 to $800,000
- $800,000 to $1 million
- $1 million and higher

Carrying Costs Budget

(combined monthly HOA fees & golf dues)

YOUR HOME SEARCH CHECKLIST

Choose One

- $100 to $250
- $250 to $400
- $400 to $550
- $550 to $750
- $750 to $1,000
- $1,000 and over

Narrow Location by State

(rank preferences)

Virginia

- Coastal
- Inland (no water)
- Lake
- Mountains

North Carolina

- Coastal
- Inland (no water)
- Lake
- Mountains

South Carolina

- Coastal
- Inland (no water)
- Lake
- Mountains

Georgia

- Coastal
- Inland (no water)
- Lake
- Mountains

Florida

- Coastal
- Inland (no water)
- Lake

Other State

- Type of geography

Desired In-Community Services

(rank in order of your preferences)

- Guarded Entrance Gate
- Electronic Entrance Gate
- Tennis
- Pickleball
- Fitness Center
- Walking Trails
- Social Clubs
- Personal Golf Carts permitted on roads, course
- Golf course that permits walking
- Pool(s)—indoor and/or outdoor
- Equestrian Center
- Marina
- Dog Park

YOUR HOME SEARCH CHECKLIST

Desired Nearby Services

(within five miles; rank in order of preferences)
- Commercial airport
- Supermarket(s)
- Restaurant(s)
- Retail shopping
- Hospital/medical facilities & offices
- Culture (museums, theaters)
- College/university (adult education, sporting events)
- Access to beach
- Access to lake

GLORIOUS BACK NINE

Acknowledgements

Too many cooks may spoil the broth, but I have had some outstanding chefs in the creative kitchen with me during the production of this book, about 15 years in the making.

Although I used my first word processing program in 1980, I am all thumbs when it comes to the sophisticated technologies of authoring programs and how to get a book published these days. I am indebted to Anneliese Fox, an author herself, for walking me through the minefields of today's technology.

My son Tim has been obsessed with golf, in all its idiosyncratic glories, since the age of 6. It led him to a high school and collegiate golf career and, finally, to a job in the industry with the Golf Channel. His editorial assistance was fundamental to getting the book to its publishable status. (A solid return on my wife's and my investment in his university English degree.)

Over the last 15 years, I have received quite an education about golf communities and real estate, and I owe much to the wisdom and council of developers, real estate professionals, general managers, golf professionals and board members in some of the Southeast Region's great golf communities. I hope their patience with my probing questions has been rewarded in the previous pages. A special thanks to veteran developer, attorney and consultant Ken Kirkman of Carolina Colours in New Bern, NC, whom I have pestered with many questions over the last decade. He has raised my golf community IQ. And to Brad Klein, a noted golf writer, whose comments helped keep my prose from landing in the rough spots. Golf architect John LaFoy designed one of the first golf community courses I visited, and one of my favorites, Glenmore outside Charlottesville,

VA. He was exceedingly generous with his time, input and unique perspective during the final stages of editing the book.

New and old friends were equally generous and essential to helping me across the finish line. Brad Chambers is a golf partner and fellow blogger who understands the interests and challenges of the senior golfer, and demonstrates that at his site ShootingYourAge.com; and Brett Miller, a new friend and veteran golf industry consultant and real estate professional, who validated some of my more aggressive contentions and keyed me into some emerging trends among golf community golfers. My longest enduring friend, Janet Feldman, doesn't know much about golf, but she knows the meaning and power of words. An accomplished writer, she gave my draft its most scrupulous reading and saved me from myself in a number of spots. Thanks, old friend.

Most of all, this book is the direct product of the hundreds of conversations with clients and friends I have met through my blog site. They have taught me as much about how to search for a golf home as, I hope, I have shared with them. Thank you to all but especially to Steve Benz, whose scrupulous reading of an early draft pointed out some fundamental embellishments about the search for a golf home; and to Andy Litteral, whose friendship, golf course camaraderie and smart reading of my first draft inspired and refined my efforts. And, of course, to my book cover models, Richard and Lisa Liberth, who graciously permitted me to display their classic swings.

Last but not least, my wife Connie has shared our nearly 40 years together with my seductive mistresses—the golf course and my laptop computer—without complaint or demand. For the last 15 years, she has indulged my "retirement boondoggle" by which she means my excuse for golf travel. For her patience and support, no author could be more grateful to his muse.

ACKNOWLEDGEMENTS

Index

55+ community *45*

A

advisory committee *62*
age-restricted communities *44*
Aiken *13, 48, 65, 66, 118, 119*
AirBnB *70*
Alabama *6, 20, 21*
ambassador program *52*
amenities *5, 16, 22, 26, 38, 51, 54, 60, 63, 64, 79, 92, 101, 122*
Arizona *7, 8*
Arnold Palmer *95, 96, 97, 102, 105, 109, 111, 113, 120, 123, 126*
Arthur Hills *96, 109, 112, 119, 120, 126, 127, 129*
Asheville *12, 13, 48, 106*
assessments *54, 117*
Atlanta *18, 38, 42, 124*
Augusta *17, 101, 119*
Ault, Clark & Associates *103*

B

Bald Head Island *19, 101*
beach *12, 22, 26, 43, 69, 71, 95, 99, 101, 108, 109, 110, 112, 120, 125, 139*
Best Places *29, 131*
Best Place to Retire *29*
Bill Love *99, 103*
Bob Moore *104*
bocce *24, 28*
bugs *56*
bundled membership *62*
buyer's real estate agent *33*
bylaws *43*

C

California *21*
capital reserves *60*
Carolinas *6, 8, 11, 12, 14, 20, 43, 76, 79, 108*
carrying costs *9, 40, 63, 72, 92*
Chapel Hill *12, 13, 85, 100, 104*
Charleston *4, 13, 14, 18, 26, 42, 55, 79, 109, 110, 111*
Charlotte *18, 42, 103*
checklist *89*
choosing a home *87, 88*
Clemson University *77*
ClubCorp *48, 49, 96, 97, 114, 118, 124*
club governance *61*
club membership *iii, 23, 40, 59, 62, 63, 64, 67, 68, 83, 116*
club newsletter *66*
Clyde Johnston *101, 110*
coast *6, 8, 12, 13, 14, 16, 19, 26, 41, 43, 69, 74, 76, 80, 99, 109*
CoMagine Health *29*
commercial airport *22*
commission *32, 33*
Condo associations *73*
Condominium ownership *42*
Condominiums *73*
construction costs *83, 136*
continuing education *8*
cost of living *3, 8, 10, 20, 21, 28, 29, 131*
cost of new home construction *82*
covenants *53, 60, 62*
Covid-19 *2, 3, 6, 64, 84*
croquet *24, 28*
customer testimonials *26*

D

Dan Maples *96, 99, 106*
Davis Love III *104, 112, 118*
developer *27, 32, 36, 53, 54, 60, 61, 62, 64, 65, 82, 99, 100, 115, 129, 141*
discounted green fee *68*
Discovery Package *51, 92*
Dual-Season Resort Areas *71*
due diligence *36, 61, 85*

E

Eastern Carolina State University *77*
Ed Carton *98*
Ellis Maples *98, 104*
equity membership *59, 60*

F

financial reserves *36, 53, 73*
financials *37*
fitness center *22, 26, 67*
Florida *6, 8, 12, 14, 15, 20, 21, 24, 25, 26, 29, 35, 42, 71, 72, 105, 106, 107, 124, 138*
  Jacksonville *13, 18, 26, 121, 124*
  Stuart *72, 126*
Fred Couples *102, 104*
full-golf membership *23, 64*

G

geography *8, 9, 37, 75, 92, 138*
George Cobb *101, 105, 110, 112, 114, 117*
Georgia *6, 8, 12, 16, 20, 21, 26, 38, 41, 48, 76, 80, 88, 120, 138*
  Greensboro *38*
golf cart *5*
golf communities *55, 63–142*
  Belfair Plantation *63, 113*
  Berkeley Hall Plantation *63*
  Brunswick Forest *37, 38, 100*
  Caledonia Golf & Fish Club *68*
  Callawassie Island *88, 89, 111*
  Carolina Colours *82, 99, 141*
  Champion Hills *36, 37, 106*
  Cliffs communities *41, 47, 54, 64, 65, 114, 117, 118, 120*
  Colleton River Club *63, 64*
  Cypress Landing *76, 77, 103*
  DeBordieu Colony *43, 44, 76, 109*
  Governors Club *85, 100*
  Haig Point *19*
  Keowee Key *54, 77, 78, 114*
  Kiawah Island *65, 110, 111*
  Landfall *41, 42, 100*
  Pawleys Plantation *42, 43, 58, 59, 69, 108*
  Porters Neck Plantation *41*
  Reynolds Lake Oconee *37, 38, 48, 122*
  The Landings *16, 41, 48, 54, 120*
  The Reserve at Lake Keowee *54, 114*
  Willoughby Country Club *72*
golf community living *58*
GolfCommunityReviews.com *6, 10, 23*
Golf CommunityReviews Questionnaire *23*
golf fees *40, 92, 103*
golf groups *66*
golf initiation fee *27, 39*
Google Maps *26, 132*
grandchildren *6, 18, 19, 72*
Greenville *4, 7, 13, 17, 18, 41, 42, 55, 77, 103, 104, 115, 116, 117, 118*
Gulfstream *14*

H

Hale Irwin *101*
high tide *79, 80*
Hilton Head *19, 40, 111, 112, 113, 114*
Home On The Course *66*
homeowner association *9, 23, 28, 31, 71, 72*
Homeowner association *16*
homesites *24, 64, 83, 84, 126, 128*

ACKNOWLEDGEMENTS

hospital *16, 22, 24, 55, 108*
hurricanes *13, 14, 53*

I

inland golf communities *75*
Insure.com *29*
Internet *9, 22, 25, 26, 29, 92*
island *19, 101, 110, 113, 127*

J

Jack Nicklaus *42, 48, 63, 78, 85, 95, 96, 100, 103, 104, 106, 108, 110, 112, 114, 122, 123, 125, 126*
Jerry Kamis *98*
Jim Anthony *65*
Joe Lee *106, 124, 125, 126, 129*
John LaFoy *97*

K

Ken Kirkman *82, 141*
Kiplinger *20, 29, 131*

L

lake *11, 17, 22, 48, 75, 76, 77, 78, 79, 92, 97, 105, 114, 119, 128, 139*
Lake Thurmond *17, 78*
lake views *75, 77*
Lee Trevino *103*
Lennar *62, 127, 128*
Lester George *97*
lifestyle *2, 3, 6, 8, 9, 16, 32, 55, 92*
Lord Baltimore Capital *38*
Low Country *6, 76, 79, 80, 122*

M

management fee *71*
mandatory membership *62*
marshland *48, 76, 79, 123*
marsh views *43, 80*
membership costs *27*
Metropolitan Life Insurance *38, 122*
Mississippi *21, 29*

monthly dues *23, 40, 48, 54, 63, 68*
mosquitoes *56*
mountains *6, 7, 8, 11, 12, 26, 76, 92, 105, 118, 123*
multi-course communities *22, 47*
multi-course memberships *67*
Multiple Listing Service *32*
Myrtle Beach *13, 14, 18, 44, 60, 71, 76, 80, 101, 107, 108*

N

Naples *12, 13, 128, 129*
National Hurricane Center *13, 14, 15*
Nerdwallet.com *4, 10, 132*
New England *4, 72*
new home *24, 81, 82, 83, 85*
Nicklaus Design *101, 104, 105, 118*
no-income-tax states *20*
non-equity *59, 60*
non-equity private club *59*
non-golfers *6, 58*
non-refundable initiation fee *60*

O

ocean *11, 13, 22, 26, 69, 75, 76, 77, 80, 99, 110, 112, 125*

P

pandemic *2, 36, 84*
P.B. Dye *101, 115, 116*
personal residence *70*
Pete Dye *43, 63, 96, 100, 108, 109, 110, 112, 121, 124, 125*
pickle ball *24, 28*
Pinehurst *7, 11, 47, 76, 103*
pluff (plough) mud *79*
POA *36*
pools *5, 22, 23, 43, 45, 67, 101, 129*
private golf communities *40*
Property Owner Association *36*
property tax *3, 4, 7, 20, 28, 40, 71*
public option *68*

R

Raleigh *18, 42, 101*
Real estate *31, 32, 76, 104*
real estate agent *28, 32, 36*
real estate agents *32, 33, 39, 41, 88, 89, 92*
real estate management company *70*
recession *2, 38, 39, 48, 54, 59, 60, 63, 64, 65, 67, 84, 97, 102, 114, 119, 121, 123, 129*
Rees Jones *48, 98, 99, 109, 110, 111, 122, 127*
Rental properties *71*
resale homes *82, 88*
resort communities *43*
retiree-friendly taxes *21*
retirement *2, 3, 6, 18, 20, 23, 24, 25, 29, 47, 72, 131, 132, 142*
Rick Robbins *102, 126*
Ritz Carlton *48*
rural golf communities *72*

S

Sales taxes *20*
Savannah *4, 13, 14, 16, 17, 18, 26, 41, 42, 48, 54, 78, 119, 120, 121, 123*
semi-private club *58, 104*
short-term rentals *43, 70*
single-family homes *42, 43, 102, 107, 121, 126*
social clubs *49, 67*
social membership *23, 65, 67*
Social Security income *20*
South Street Partners *65*
state income tax *20*
Sunset *55, 101, 114*
supermarket *17, 22, 24*

T

Tampa *18*
Tennessee *6, 20, 21, 76, 98, 108*
tennis *26, 129*
The Carolinas *6*
  North Carolina
    Chocowinity *76, 77, 103*
    Hendersonville *36, 37, 106*
    New Bern *82, 99, 141*
    Pamlico River *77, 103*
    Sandhills *7, 11, 76*
    Southport *19, 101*
    Wrightsville Beach *41*
  South Carolina *19, 20, 21, 29, 41, 43, 48, 54, 69, 77, 88, 106, 107, 111, 115, 137*
    Bluffton *40, 63, 64, 84, 111, 112, 113*
    Daufuskie Island *19*
    Georgetown *43, 44, 76, 109*
    Hilton Head *19, 40, 111, 112, 113, 114*
    Lake Keowee *41, 54, 77, 78, 114*
    McCormick *17, 78, 119*
    Okatie *88, 89, 111*
    Pawleys Island *42, 56, 59, 68, 69, 73, 108*
    Salem *77*
    Seneca *69*
The Landings on Skidaway Island *16*
Tim Cate *100, 101*
Tom Fazio *41, 63, 96, 98, 100, 103, 105, 106, 108, 110, 111, 112, 113, 114, 115, 117, 120, 122, 124, 128*
Topography *8*
TopRetirements.com *9*
townhouse *43*
Troon *48, 49, 118*

U

United Van Lines Survey Results *9, 131*

V

vacation home *29, 56, 69, 70, 71, 73, 74, 121*
Virginia *6, 12, 13, 21, 26, 95, 97, 137*
  Richmond *42, 121*
VRBO *70*

W

walking trails *5, 22, 26*
waterfront lots *77, 78*
water view *75, 76*
website *15, 23, 26, 27, 43*
wellness center *38*
Where to Retire *28*
Willard Byrd *101, 111, 113, 120, 127*
Wilmington *13, 14, 18, 26, 38, 41, 42, 100, 101, 102*
wooded lots *75*
Woodside Plantation *48, 65, 66, 118*

www.ingramcontent.com/pod-product-compliance
Lightning Source LLC
Chambersburg PA
CBHW070908080526
44589CB00013B/1219